YORKSHIRE'S
PREHISTORIC
MONUMENTS

First published 2023

The History Press
97 St George's Place, Cheltenham,
Gloucestershire, GL50 3QB
www.thehistorypress.co.uk

British Library Cataloguing in Publication Data.
A catalogue record for this book is available from the British Library.

ISBN 978 1 8039 9106 1

Printed and bound in Great Britain by TJ Books Limited, Padstow, Cornwall.

Trees for LYfe

MIX
Paper from
responsible sources
FSC® C013056

YORKSHIRE'S PREHISTORIC MONUMENTS

Written & illustrated by

ADAM MORGAN IBBOTSON

ACKNOWLEDGEMENTS

Back in the autumn of 2019 I was sifting through old photos, editing a few I took of Castlerigg Stone Circle for print. During that fateful period of editing, I conjured up the idea of creating a simple guidebook for the public, detailing each prehistoric monument in the Lake District. Over 300 prehistoric sites, a nationwide lockdown, and 80,000 words later, I can confidently say that I have learned a thing-or-two about English pre-history... Even then, there remains much to learn. This is made abundantly clear as I reflect upon the individuals who have helped and supported me over the past four years.

First and foremost, I express my sincere gratitude to the numerous academics who have generously assisted me. Whether through casual conversations or persistent email inquiries, their guidance and support have been invaluable. I extend special appreciation to Mark Brennand of Cumbria County Council, whose expertise and willingness to respond to my queries fuelled my thirst for knowledge. Additionally, archaeologist and all-around great man Peter Style, graciously proofread my first book and imparted a wealth of information in the process. I am particularly indebted to my university supervisor Professor Kevin Walsh, whose

teachings significantly enriched my understanding of prehistoric landscapes. I must also thank David R. Abram and Mary-Ann Ochota for their support of this book. Their remarkable contributions to the field of popular archaeology have deeply influenced me in recent years.

I am of course also thankful for the assistance from my friends and family during the creation of my two books. Their unwavering encouragement and support played a significant role in my journey. Field trips became unforgettable with the companionship of my friends Jamie Booth, Matt Staniek, Chris Shreiber, and Jay A. There was also the support of my wonderful partner Keziah, as well as my parents Ian and Glynis. All these people were essential in visiting many of the sites featured in this book, joining me on ventures along rain drenched country roads and boggy moors in search of the most isolated of sites. I would also be remiss not to express overdue gratitude to Elsa Price, Marnie Calvert, and Professor Terence Meaden for their early contributions and support, which greatly enriched my first book, *Cumbria's Prehistoric Monuments*.

CONTENTS

We might imagine limits to a difficult landscape;
see grikes and clints stitched by bold saplings.

We might value history's deep mulch, know the
economy of stones; balky vaults of old memory.

An excerpt from 'An Economy of Stones' by Simon De Courcey.

INTRODUCTION

The prehistoric monuments of Britain offer a remarkable glimpse into the daily life and religious practices of Europe's earliest settled communities. They are the remnants of cultures that inhabited the British Isles during two distinct periods: the **Neolithic** and the **Bronze Age**, between 4000 BC and 700 BC. This span of time could be seen as a prehistoric golden age, thousands of years before the arrival of the Romans. It was during this epoch that some of Europe's grandest monuments were created.

Despite the appreciation such monuments garner, the public generally recognises only a few sites. Stonehenge, for instance, has long been the global mascot for the Stone Age. Likewise, there are regions of Britain synonymous with prehistory. Orkney, Wiltshire, Cornwall and the Lake District are often discussed in relation to Britain's prehistoric past. Indeed, of the thousands of stone monuments strewn across our countryside, it seems the majority exist at the isles' western extremities. But this does not represent the full picture. Eastern England, particularly the area encompassing the historic counties of Yorkshire, saw the emergence of prehistoric cultures capable of creating vast, complex and often mind-bogglingly grand monuments.

Although most of Yorkshire's population resides in cities, much of the county remains rural. The region's upland moors, for instance, stretching from Whitby to Ingleton, have been perfect for the preservation of prehistoric monuments.

With a smaller population density, less land was swallowed by housing developments, trading estates and roads. In such areas, monuments both large and small have survived in relative isolation for upwards of 5,000 years. Among these are ancient landmarks, seldom found elsewhere in Europe, their rarity a result of their survival in the face of adversity.

Yorkshire has many beautiful landscapes, from the North York Moors to the limestone crags of the Dales. It is a county as rich in human history as other regions in the UK but its tales are often untold, its stories unwritten. Despite this lack of attention, the land is alive with the echoes of the past, as Yorkshire covers a vast expanse encompassing hundreds of treasures from prehistoric times. So, while the author of this book cannot provide an exhaustive list of sites in Yorkshire, this book will detail the majority of viewable and visitable prehistoric landmarks.

With standing stones taller than those in Wiltshire, burial monuments grander than those in the Lake District, and rock art more abundant than much of Europe, Yorkshire deserves to be acknowledged as the archaeological Eden it is. In this book, you will find an assortment of monuments, some on the tourist trail and others that are virtually unknown. You may find the best sites lay off the beaten track, in the most unexpected areas, which is terrific if you enjoy an adventure into the unfamiliar. I invite you to take a journey thousands of years back into our past, to an era sculpted by ancient hands.

These are **Yorkshire's Prehistoric Monuments**.

A QUICK GUIDE
BEFORE YOU START

Since the seventeenth century, academics and institutions across Europe have worked to further our understanding of Europe's prehistoric past. When speculating upon relatively simple stone arrangements, it was oftentimes necessary to coin new terms to differentiate between sites. Therefore, an archaeological jargon has emerged. Take the paragraph below as an example:

'The **megaliths** serve as a **kerb** around the **barrow**. At the centre of this **chambered cairn** is a **cist** covered by a **capstone**. Decorated with **cup and ring markings**, its position at the end of the **cursus crop mark** makes it the perfect spot to view the **Class II henge**.'

If you understand this paragraph, you should turn the page and continue. But for the uninitiated, please do take note of the small glossary on the following page.

Throughout this book, the author will explain the historical context behind these sites and their proposed functions. There may be times when it is necessary to refer to this glossary, and that is without shame. Despite appearing crude on their surface, these monuments are vestiges of a complex prehistoric society we have yet to fully understand.

In describing these sites, the author will be crediting those who have studied and explored Yorkshire's prehistoric monuments. However, there may be times when phrases along the lines of 'some speculate' and 'many have theorised' are used. In such cases, complex multi-source theories are condensed into small summaries for the sake of easy readability. The sources for such theories are written in the bibliography at the back of the book, which lists all texts referenced, as well as the databases accessed during research.

Indeed, this book does not endeavour to attach undeniable dates and answers to each of the monuments listed. Instead, it aims to provide information on what is known about each site, and the theories this has produced. I would advise the academically inclined among the readership to explore the avenues of my research by checking my sources.

> **Author's Note:** Often, prehistoric monuments are situated in hard to access areas, be it physically or legally. This book serves to inform the reader of the extent of the prehistoric monuments in Yorkshire; it is not an invitation to trespass on or disturb any of the areas detailed in its pages. Do not trample cairns, do not lift stones, and do not use metal detectors at these sites; doing so is against the law, and is generally frowned upon. Do not do it.

TERM	DEFINITION
Barrow	Any variety of mound intended to inter the dead. Same as a 'tumulus'.
Bell beaker	A non-funerary pottery vessel dating to the Early Bronze Age, typically 12–30cm tall with a fluted top.
Burial cairn	A mound of stones created to mark burials.
Burial circle	A stone circle with a central burial cairn.
Cairn-field	An expanse of land with several prehistoric cairns.
Cap stone	A stone that covers a cist burial.
Cist	A small, stone-built coffin-like box or ossuary used to hold the bodies of the dead. Typically found within burial cairns.
Concentric stone circle	At least one stone circle encircling another.
Crag	A steep or rugged cliff or rock face.
Cremation cemetery	An area where bodies were cremated and buried, either in coffins or cists.
Crop marks	Patterns found in crop fields, due to differing levels of soil depth. Lighter marks are caused by shallow soils, darker marks signify trenches or pits.

Cup and ring marks	A style of rock art typical of the early to mid-Neolithic (3800–2750 BC) consisting of chiselled rings and dots on a rockface.
Cursus monument	Vast, cigar-shaped earthen enclosures created near the beginning of the Neolithic (est. 3800 BC).
Dyke	A man-made trench, often used in prehistoric and medieval times to delineate land boundaries.
Flint	A form of quartz used throughout the stone age to sculpt cutting tools.
Henge	An earthwork typical of the Neolithic period, consisting of a roughly circular or oval-shaped bank with an internal ditch surrounding a central flat area.
Hut circle	The foundation of a prehistoric roundhouse, typically circular stone walls with a single entrance and a cobbled interior.
Kerb stones	Stones holding a mound of stone or earth in place around its outside.
Polished axe	A well-honed stone axe typically dating to the Neolithic period, although earlier examples have been found.
Portal	A term used to define large stones that appear to form an entrance.
Solstice	The day when the sun reaches its highest point. This occurs twice a year, in summer and winter, marking both the longest (summer) and shortest (winter) days of the year.
Stone avenue	Two rows of stone erected parallel within the landscape.
Stone circle	A circular arrangement of stones.
Stone row	A single row of stones that forms a line in the landscape.
Survivor's bias	A logical error made by concentrating on items that survive today, ignoring non-surviving examples.
Tumulus/tumuli	Any variety of mound intended to inter the dead. Same as a 'barrow'.

MOUND VARIETY	DESCRIPTION
Kerbed barrow	A style of burial monument common in the Early Bronze Age (2500–1800 BC). A circle of stones around the base of a mound of earth or stone.
Bowl barrow	An earth-covered tomb with a resemblance to an upturned bowl (3200 BC–AD 700).
Clearance cairn	An uneven heap of stones removed from farmland. Does not contain burials.
Long barrow	A long earthen tumulus. Typically made during the early Neolithic (4000–3200 BC).
Long cairn	A rare long stone tumulus. Made during the early Neolithic (3800–3200 BC).
Passage tomb	A mid-Neolithic burial mound, with a narrow access passage made of large stones (3400–2800 BC).
Ring cairn	A circular enclosure made from loose stones, can be kerbed. Sometimes known as 'cremation cemeteries'. If topped with a stone circle, they are known as 'embanked stone circles'.
Round cairn	Large stone mounds covering single or multiple burials. Typically made during the Bronze Age (2500–800 BC).

THE NEOLITHIC – 4200–2500 BC

NEO: NEW OR OF RECENT MANUFACTURE.

LITHIC: OF THE NATURE OF OR RELATING TO STONE.

There is ceaseless debate about what defines the Neolithic, and when the period began. As such, please forgive the abridged theory below. This is a complicated topic, wrapped up in archaeological, scientific and philosophical debate, with plenty left to learn.

Around 6200 BC, the world warmed. Wildfires swept through Europe, and land once dominated by forests became clear and fertile. Over the next several centuries, populations fleeing a drought-ridden Near East slowly migrated west. They brought innovative farming techniques, fixed settlements and complex religious systems with them. By 4200 BC, the French and Spanish coasts were already home to monument-building cultures. Britain, on the other hand, remained largely wild, and was among the last regions in Western Europe permanently settled by farming communities.

Prehistoric monuments first emerged in Yorkshire in the 'early Neolithic' period (est. 4000–3200 BC). During this era, vast elongated enclosures called cursus monuments were built across the region's lowlands. Large communal burial mounds, such as long barrows, long cairns and bank cairns were built on adjacent hillsides.

People had yet to dominate the British landscape in the early Neolithic, and most of it remained forested. Early Neolithic monuments often demonstrate an emphasis on nearby landscape features, suggesting that views of distant landscapes may have been obstructed by woodland. However, with the dawn of agriculture and fixed settlement, it was only a matter of time before people would begin to clear the British landscape.

Neolithic people cleared many forests in Britain. This was a crucial necessity, as they would need to repeatedly relocate and clear forests in pursuit of fertile soils. At the same time, the previous inhabitants of the British Isles – the 'Mesolithic hunter-gatherers' (est. 8000–4000 BC) – saw a steep decline in population. Still, it seems early Neolithic farmers lived and bred with these early folk. DNA evidence, collected from long barrows, has shown Mesolithic genetics survived as a form of 'elite'. Inbreeding to preserve their lineages, Neolithic society may have been dynastic. This is further evident in early Neolithic artefacts, which appear to have been passed down through generations. For example, Early Neolithic 'Langdale stone axes' from the Lake District (est. 3400 BC) have been found deposited within much later burials in Yorkshire, sometimes as late as the Early Bronze Age (a gap of over a thousand years).

As the era advanced into the mid to late Neolithic period, spanning from 3200 BC to 2500 BC, the use of megalithic standing stones increased, and the design of enclosures shifted towards a circular shape. These enclosures are believed to have served as religious ceremonial centres, as they were often aligned towards the solstice sun. During this era, burial monuments also underwent a change, adopting a round shape and featuring chambers capable of accommodating multiple bodies. The practice of interring disarticulated skeletons, where limbs were removed prior to burial, was prevalent during this period. As a result, Neolithic burial chambers are frequently found to contain an assortment of jumbled bones. People later removed bones from these graves to use in rituals.

Rock art is another indicator of the Neolithic period. Neolithic motifs, such as cup and ring marks (est. 3600–3200 BC) and passage tomb art (est. 3200–2800 BC), were common across northern England. Many stone circles, cairns, natural outcrops and burial chambers exhibit cup and ring marks. Examples of passage tomb art are rarer in Yorkshire, but they can be found carved onto some megalithic tombs overlooking the coast. Yorkshire contains one of the densest collections of Neolithic rock art in Europe. It is therefore crucial to our understanding of its context.

THE EARLY BRONZE AGE – 2500–1600 BC

BRONZE: AN ALLOY METAL CONSISTING PRIMARILY OF COPPER AND TIN. **AGE**: A DISTINCT PERIOD OF HISTORY.

The Early Bronze Age was a continuation of the Neolithic period and signalled the end of the Stone Age, marking the beginning of significant cultural advancements in Britain. It was not a sudden or definite event, but rather a gradual transition as metalworking techniques spread across Europe through migration and trade. Despite its name, the Bronze Age was a time of increase in all metal production, leading to a surge in the creation of bronze, copper and gold artefacts.

At the conclusion of the Neolithic era, Britain was witness to a cataclysmic event. Once thriving Neolithic farming communities underwent a significant decline, and it is estimated that as much as 90 per cent of the population was replaced by newcomers. The cause of this sudden change remains shrouded in mystery, as it is unclear whether it was a result of famine, disease or even acts of genocide. Genetic evidence of the Neolithic farmers was erased in some regions. Yet, interestingly, stone arrangements from the Early Bronze Age continued to exhibit a similar complexity. For example, the construction of Stonehenge began during the Neolithic, but it underwent a significant renovation during this pivotal transitional period, with its lintels being lifted and repositioned.

While pottery making did begin in earnest during the Neolithic, the dawn of the Early Bronze Age would kickstart a revolution in how pots were created. Bronze Age migrants introduced bell beakers, decorated vessels shaped like church bells. Believed to have developed in Iberia, in a region near modern-day Portugal, the bell beaker would come to dominate Western Europe. These vessels are linked to the so-called Beaker People. Genetic evidence has shown these people to have migrated westwards from Eastern Europe, possibly adopting the beaker from an invasion of Iberia around 2900 BC. By 2500 BC, these warlike people had arrived in Britain, bringing their beaker, their warfare, their language and their metallurgy with them.

Despite their strong ties to their respective styles of pottery, nobody knows the purpose of Early Bronze Age beakers. Flared around their opening and with a narrow base, they are distinct from other pots. They are not often found to contain cremated remains but are instead buried next to the deceased, empty. One popular theory suggests these vessels were beer jugs, placed beside the deceased to be carried over to a boozy afterlife. Indeed, this style of burial is a telltale sign of Beaker activity, having a body buried in a foetal position, often next to flint or bronze weapons and beakers. These are known as Beaker burials. Partly due to these lavish burial practices, researchers believe this period was lorded over by powerful chieftains or religious elites.

Despite the cultural chaos, iconic prehistoric sites saw much activity during this period. Like the Victorian era's 'Gothic Revival', inspired by medieval architecture, the Early Bronze Age saw something of a megalithic revival. Many stone circles began their creation during the Neolithic but had their largest stones raised during the Early Bronze Age. Indeed, the cultures that settled in the British Isles would go on to inherit its traditions.

THE MID TO LATE BRONZE AGE – 1600–1000 BC

The mid to late Bronze Age was a major, if less dramatic, turning point in Britain's timeline. It seems that by 1600 BC, community-led megalithic construction had ceased. Instead, mid-Bronze Age people were seemingly focused on everyday domestic activities – the important things in life: food, safety and shelter. The most common archaeological sites relating to this period are farming settlements and boundary earthworks. Unfortunately, due to the absence of any written records from the period, the cause of this momentous cultural shift remains unknown.

However, using comparisons to world history, it would seem a change in social structure may have been to blame. The Mayans of Central America, for instance, saw the emergence of their 'Golden Age' (AD 600) when ruled by powerful, idolised leaders. Britain would also be graced with villas, roads and massive defensive structures with the arrival of the Roman Empire in AD 43. In both cases, the collapse of a dominant social hierarchy led to the mass abandonment of construction projects and a void in the archaeological record (i.e., the Mayan Collapse or the Dark Ages). Indeed, powerful empires sometimes fall like dominoes, dragging everything down with them. For the British Bronze Age, this may have translated to fewer chieftains dictating what people should, or could, do. Therefore, fewer large-scale ceremonial monuments were constructed.

The mid-Bronze Age in Yorkshire saw a gradual increase in small, individual burials. Unlike earlier graves, which often contained lavish burial goods, such as weapons or jewellery, mid-Bronze Age graves tend to be more restrained. Individual burials became more common, and rather than large mounds, burial urns were placed in pits without a cist. These urns are often found in designated areas, known as 'urnfields', hallowed grounds comparable to modern graveyards. Interestingly, Bronze Age urnfields are sometimes located near or within Neolithic sites, indicating a continuation of beliefs and practices over time.

6000 Years Ago

EARLY
NEOLITHIC
4000 BC - 3200 BC

- Cursus Monuments

- Long Barrows / Long Cairns

- Cup and Ring Marks

- Polished Stone Axes

5200 Years Ago

MID-TO-LATE
NEOLITHIC
3200 BC - 2500 BC

Henges -

Passage Tomb Art -

Stone Circles / Rows -

Mortuary Enclosures -

4500 Years Ago

EARLY
BRONZE AGE
2500 BC - 1800 BC

- Beaker Pottery

- Round Barrows / Cairns

- Ring Cairns

- Cairnfields

3800 Years Ago

MID-TO-LATE
BRONZE AGE
1800 BC - 700 BC

- Upland Settlements
- Burial Urns in Pits
- Dykes
- Hill Forts

CHAPTER ONE

NORTH YORK MOORS

The North York Moors encompass 885km of hilly terrain, stretching from the A19 to Whitby. This expanse was formed over thousands of years, when glaciers scooped out wide valleys in the sandstone geology. Millennia of erosion shaped the rolling hills and vast valleys into a fertile highland region, with dense forests covering the hills. However, as evidenced by the swathes of barren moorland we see today, something changed.

During the Mesolithic era, when people relied on hunting and gathering, the moors remained lush with woodland. That was until 4000 BC, with the arrival of the early Neolithic, when England's woodlands began to vanish. From that point on, the modern moorlands we know today took shape. People cleared the woodlands to create pastures and piled natural rocks into clearance cairns, forming vast cairn-fields to make room for ploughing. They reshaped the land like never before, making it habitable for pasture. This deforestation only accelerated during the Bronze Age, as the climate favoured settlement at higher altitudes.

Ironically, this sculpting in pursuit of farmable land is why these hills are seldom inhabited today. Millennia of decaying biomaterial from lost natural habitats have rendered the moor's soils acidic, leaving only the hardiest plants and animals to thrive. It is for this reason that prehistoric monuments have survived so well across the national park. Urban development, for the most part, has veered far from the moors. Aside from the odd military base or stone cross, the Moors are something of a time capsule.

BILSDALE AND RAISDALE

Our journey commences in the picturesque Bilsdale and Raisdale Valleys, the westernmost access points into the North York Moors. Sitting between the Hambleton Hills and heights of Urra Moor, these are among the most sheltered of the North York Moors' valleys. However, the same cannot be said for the prehistoric monuments in the region, which were built along the uplands. The majority of these are Early Bronze Age burial mounds, built in rows along the crests of the moors. Round cairns, circular stone-built burial mounds, are particularly prevalent in Bilsdale.

Wholton Moor, Live Moor, Cringle Moor and Cold Moor are all dotted with round cairns, which are found in rows aligned towards the solstice sunrise/sunset. Rows of burial mounds are believed to have not only aligned to points in the landscape or sky, but also to have marked boundaries in the landscape between communities.

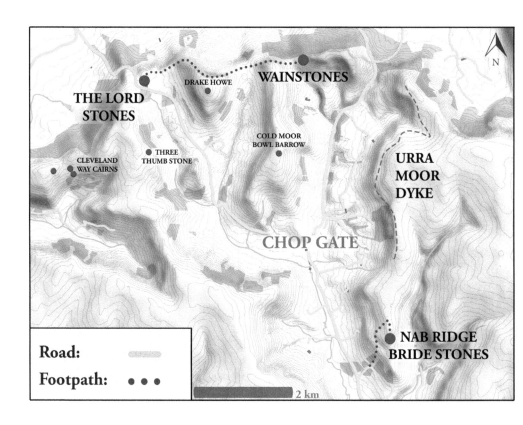

Certainly, social boundaries were important to Bronze Age people, and were made obvious in the landscape. A clear boundary, the Urra Moor Dyke, marks the crest of Urra Moor, east of Chop Gate. Dykes like this are covered in greater detail later within this chapter, but simply put: they are ditches dug to mark boundaries, often dated to the mid-Bronze Age (est. 1600–700 BC). Accessing the dyke is easy, as its length is followed by a footpath.

THE LORD STONES

NZ 52368 02980

Two small mounds can be seen poking up from an unkempt field in the west of Lord Stones Country Park, near the brow of Green Bank. Although they may appear unremarkable at first glance, these mounds are two of a total of four 'round barrows' on the hillside. Such earthen mounds, built to hold the remains of the dead, are a common sight throughout the national park, particularly along its outer edges. At least eight round barrows dot the uplands surrounding Green Bank, but those closest to the country park are the most visible and accessible of them all.

The barrow nearest the road is surrounded by kerb stones, which hold the mound in place. These are the eponymous Lord Stones, which lend their name to the adjacent visitors' centre. The largest of these, known as the Three Lord Stone, is decorated with cup marks, concave depressions pecked into the surface of the rock. Cup marks typically date to the Neolithic and were likely created using stone or bone chisels.

Thousands of stone surfaces in the British Isles display cup markings, from natural crags to standing stones. Cup marks were common in northern England around the early to mid-Neolithic period (est. 3800–3000 BC), yet kerbed barrows like this

THE THREE LORD STONE AND THE DISTANT CRINGLE MOOR.

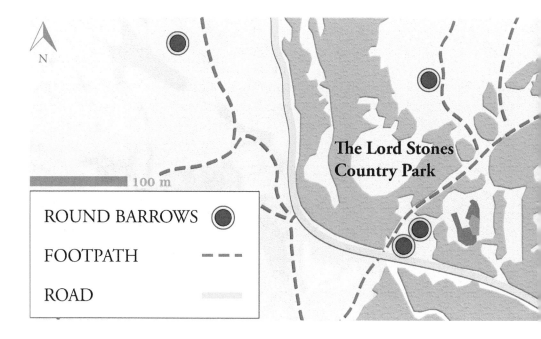

were far more abundant in the Early Bronze Age (est. 2500 BC). Therefore, the rock art may have been reused from an earlier Neolithic site, possibly a natural boulder adorned with cup marks.

The tendency for Bronze Age people to build barrows on the uplands was largely a practical matter. Weather conditions were both wetter and warmer during this time, encouraging settlement on the uplands. At this time, there developed a tendency to build barrows on the crests of hillsides, where they would silhouette against the sky, appearing larger from below. However, the position of the Lord Stones is somewhat atypical, sitting in a dip between two hills, set back from the rest.

Author's note: Although these barrows are located next to a footpath, it is important they are not disturbed. These are the final resting places of people who lived upwards of 4,500 years ago. They have endured the ravages of history only because of their isolation, which today poses them a greater risk. If you do decide to visit burial monuments like these, keep in mind that you should ideally admire from a short distance.

NAB RIDGE BRIDE STONES

SE 57565 97908

This is one of many prehistoric monuments in the North York Moors known as the 'Bride Stones', a bastardisation of the old Norse 'brink stones', meaning 'stones near a crag'. Reachable by a footpath that winds its way east from Chop Gate's village hall, the Bride Stones lie on a terrace near the edge of Nab Ridge. Though often misclassified as a stone circle, this site is, in truth, the remains of a burial mound. To the north, another round cairn survives, although it is overshadowed by a modern monument erected above it. To the north-west, down the hill, the scattered remains of a Bronze Age settlement are evident.

Twenty-seven stones form the circumference of the Bride Stones. In some areas, they are tightly arranged to create a neat ring of megaliths. Like the Lord Stones, they are kerb stones that once surrounded a mound. In England, kerb stones often disappeared first when barrows were cleared for ploughing. Yet, in this unusual case, only the rubble of the inner cairn was removed, without obvious reason.

Larger kerbed barrows like this often date to the Early Bronze Age (est. 2500 BC), built to accommodate single burials (as whole skeletons interred within cists). Not only would this example have been massive in its original form, but its prominent kerb stones suggest a fair amount of time and effort were

NAB RIDGE BRIDE STONES FROM ABOVE.

put into its creation. Sadly, much of the site was destroyed during looting, and it so it remains unclear what, or who, was buried here.

DRAKE HOWE

NZ 53754 02959

Cranimoor (or Cringle Moor), a hill between the Wainstones and the Lord Stones, has two round barrows on its crown. The largest of these, Drake Howe, is the highest burial monument in the North York Moors, overlooking breathtaking views on all sides. However, due to its somewhat small size and position at the centre of the flat-topped hill, it is not prominent from within the valley. To see it requires a hike, which is best done from the Lord Stones Country Park. As the site sits within sight of Lord Stones, only 1.2km (approximately 1 mile) away, it may be regarded as part of the same upland funerary landscape.

THREE THUMB STONE & LOW BROOMFLAT CUPS

NZ 52542 01686

Lone standing stones are rare, especially in northern England. Where they are found, as in the case of the Three Thumb Stone on Bilsdale Moor, they were likely once part of a larger monument. The stone lies on the edge of the moor, overlooking the valley to the west. It is one of several that once formed a row, now lost in the dense heather to the north. The lost row appears to have aligned towards a natural outcrop called 'Stone Ruck', which itself is adorned with a Bronze Age burial cairn.

Author's note: Several months after handing this book over to the publishers for editing, I was walking through the private land of my in-laws at Low Broomflat Farm. My partner, Keziah, had told me there was a large boulder in one of the fields, which we intended to sit on for a rest. To my complete amazement, Keziah pointed out a previously unrecorded cup-marked rock; the most complex example yet found in the valley. The boulder itself lines up with the Three Thumb Stone and Stone Ruck across the valley, aligned towards the midwinter sunset.

THE WAINSTONES

NZ 55630 03595

The Wainstones comprise a collection of rocky outcrops at the northern edge of Hasty Bank. They are the remains of a collapsed cliff face, the scree of which sprawls down the hillside to the north. It is common to find rock climbers and hikers walking the Cleveland Way here, admiring the views over the Tees Estuary and North Sea.

Neolithic people likewise took interest in the Wainstones, as many boulders in the surrounding scree fields feature rock art. These range from simple cup and ring marks to unusual geometric shapes. 'Ring markings' are a common motif at Neolithic sites in Britain. These are often found carved concentrically in groups alongside or around cup marks.

We will focus on just four carvings here, each numbered by Graeme Chappell and Paul Brown in their 2005 book, *Prehistoric Rock Art in the North York Moors*.

First, and least remarkable, is **Stone 5**, a rectangular boulder in the scree pile under the Wainstones. A single line has been pecked into its surface, trailing off the side of the boulder. Second, there is **Stone 1**, situated in the field boundary to the north. Three ring marks are etched into the top of this large slab-like boulder, alongside an impressive twenty-five cup marks. Like many rock art sites in Yorkshire, the cup marks exhibit 'tails', lines that trail out from cup marks. Third, **Stone 3**, in the field west of the Wainstones, displays a circular motif enclosing four cup marks. Motifs like this are uncommon; they are most often found on moorland boulders. Such motifs are thought to date to the Neolithic as examples have been found next to activity from that period.

LEFT:
WAINSTONES 6.

RIGHT:
WAINSTONES 3.

THE
WAINSTONES.

Finally, there is **Stone 6**, found beside the path to the south of the Wainstones. Several straight lines cut across the face of the rock, forming a large wedge or axe shape. Placed inside these lines are two cup and ring marks. There are few comparable carvings in England, but one similar example can be found on Ilkley Moor (see Chapter 3), known as **Backstones**. Such similar carvings, at such distances from each other, may suggest an esoteric meaning behind the carving – a meaning that once connected two corners of prehistoric Yorkshire.

Author's note: As you can see in my tracing, there appears to be method in the design of the motif on Stone 6. While prehistoric rock art is rarely figurative, these lines may form the outline of an axe head, the plan of a settlement or observances of the night sky.

GOATHLAND AND FYLINGDALES

The moorlands surrounding Goathland and Fylingdales are among Yorkshire's most visited upland landscapes. Judging by the surviving archaeology in the region, these moors were also a popular spot during the Neolithic and Bronze Age. A record number of burial mounds are found across the region, some small, others massive. everal landmark mid to late Neolithic (est. 3200 - 1800 BC) ceremonial monuments sit within these burial grounds, including stone rows and communal tombs. The area was evidently a hotbed of ritual activity.

The region's sea views may have motivated the construction of ritual monuments to some extent. For instance, the easternmost moors hold a high concentration of standing stones, burial mounds and ring cairns. From these easternmost uplands, you can gaze over the North Sea and witness the sunrise on the horizon – a surprisingly rare site in an upland region. For a culture that studied the skies, this may have been an ideal space for ritual activity outside the region's enclosed valley floors.

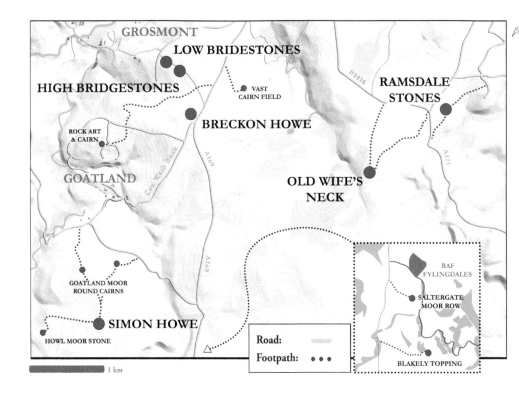

SIMON HOWE.

GOATHLAND MOOR AND SIMON HOWE

SE 83008 98096

Simon Howe is one of several large burial mounds on Goathland Moor. Unfortunately, of the six major barrows, Simon Howe, at the centre of the moor, is the most damaged. All that remains is a circle of kerb stones. While burial monuments like this are found across Yorkshire, examples this large, created using stone, are rarer.

Simon Howe is unique among the six barrows on Goathland Moor as it is the only one that has a visible kerb. The use of kerb stones, a practice associated with the Early Bronze Age period, suggests it may have been built earlier than the other barrows, closer to the Neolithic period (est. 2500 BC).

THE STONE ROW TAILING OFF FROM SIMON HOWE, LOOKING NORTH-EAST.

Given the time and effort required for its construction and its location at the centre of the moor, it is possible that Simon Howe was a very high-status burial. Other similar kerbed round cairns are found throughout the North York Moors, such as the Nab Ridge Bride Stones in Bilsdale, and Harwood Dale Circle near Burniston.

During the Early Bronze Age, multiple bodies were placed inside cairns like this, in a communal fashion. Unlike earthen barrows, which hold their primary burial within a cist below a mound, Early Bronze Age cairns like Simon Howe often hold many cists at several depths throughout their mass.

Comparable cairns are found among important ritual landscapes. A similar cairn, for example, can be found near England's third-largest stone circle, Long Meg and Her Daughters, in Glassonby, Cumbria. Simon Howe is no different, appearing to have been part of a larger megalithic complex. To the immediate north, trailing from the cairn, is a 'stone row', a linear alignment of standing stones. The row at Simon Howe is comprised of several megaliths, only four of which survive. A survey in 1947 found evidence of a missing stone in line with the others, nearer to the cairn.

The stone row implies Simon Howe may have served as more than a burial monument. Indeed, it would seem these megaliths were aligned with the solstices. Visiting the moor on a winter solstice evening, you can witness the sun set behind the kerb stones of the cairn. If the cairn had survived, the sun would have visually disappeared within its silhouette at sunset. It is anyone's guess what significance this held for the people of the Early Bronze Age, but we can assume some form of ancestor/solar worship was happening here.

The moor's four other round barrows also appear to align towards the solstices. Built in pairs, the barrows align like the crosshairs on a rifle. One pair, known as the **Two Howes**, points south-east, towards the winter solstice sunrise. The other pair, as yet unnamed, point south-west, towards the winter solstice sunset. Such alignments are typical of mid to late Neolithic and Early Bronze Age ritual complexes. These stylistic similarities may date the burial mounds on Goathland Moor to the same era, sometime between 2500 BC and 1800 BC.

THE OLD WIFE'S NECK

NZ 90067 02140

A complex of parallel ditches cuts east–west across Sneaton Low Moor, east of Fylingdales. This feature, known as Shooting House Rigg, is a cross-ridge dyke, a linear ditch with a parallel embankment running across a ridge or outcrop. Cross-ridge dykes were built in the moors from the mid-Bronze Age to the Anglo-Saxon period (est. 1700 BC–AD 800) and are thought to represent land boundaries.

It is on this cross-ridge dyke that you can find a standing stone known as the Old Wife's Neck. Its name stems from its uncanny appearance, looking like a human torso. It is one of seven stones that form a row beside the dyke.

The bank of the dyke was built around the stones, conforming to their path. It would seem the builders of the dyke were attempting to avoid the stones, suggesting they predate the dyke.

There are many theories on the purpose of stone rows, which typically date to the late Neolithic/ Early Bronze Age (est. 3000–1800 BC). They may have acted as astronomical observatories, allowing people to track the passage of the sun, moon and stars. They may have served as territorial markers, separating distinct tribes and villages. They may also have been employed in rituals and ceremonies, serving as places of gathering and veneration. The truth is likely more nuanced, with stone rows serving a multitude of purposes throughout prehistory.

Nonetheless, unlike many stone rows in northern England, which align to the solstices to the south-east or south-west, this row does not. The row, like the dyke, snakes across the ridge, aligned east to west. As the stones are unaligned to the solstices (and without other suggestions of ceremonial placement), one could suggest they did serve to delineate an Early Bronze Age land boundary, which was later re-delineated with the creation of the dyke.

HAZEL HEAD 'STONE ROW'

SE 80698 99660

This dubious collection of stones sits next to Wheeldale Roman Road, on private land next to Hazel Head Farm. It is among several perplexing features in the area, listed on OS maps as ruins, cists and piles of stone, all of which describe Roman remains. Hazel Head Stone Row is the most prominent of these features and is thought by some to be an Early Bronze Age feature. First described as 'ruins' on an 1854 map, the stones are set close together, appearing like a pair of ruinous walls. They form an east–west-aligned avenue, split in two by a modern field wall.

There has, however, been debate over the provenance of the stones. Even though they appear to form an avenue, two rows or even a wall, many believe them to be natural. Indeed, while it would seem the stones form a row, they sit among hundreds of boulders on the hillside, a natural scatter from the adjacent crags.

HIGH BRIDESTONES

NZ 85027 04614

This collection of slender standing stones survives on Sleights Moor, south of Grosmont. Not to be confused with the Nab Ridge Bride Stones near Chop Gate, the High Bridestones is a far larger and more complex arrangement of megaliths. A row of stones forms a path towards a group of six slender megaliths. This group, which we will call the South Circle, has only one megalith left standing. The circle is certainly man-made, yet difficult to decipher due to its ruinous state. One oft-repeated theory suggests the Bridestones were a stone row, ending in two stone circles. However, this hypothesis is unlikely.

THE STONE CIRCLE END OF HIGH BRIDESTONES, LOOKING SOUTH-EAST.

Antiquarian Rev. George Young visited the site in 1817. He noted:

HIGH BRIDESTONES.

> *On Sleights moor there are a remarkable assemblage ... called the High Bridestones, forming a kind of irregular line ... There were eleven upright stones in this cluster some years ago: at present there are only six standing, and three or four that have fallen down.*

Viewing the site from an aerial perspective, a clearer picture emerges. The stones of the South Circle are closely arranged, forming an enclosure 10m in diameter – too small for groups to congregate inside. Therefore, the South Circle may instead represent the showy kerb of a burial mound of some variety.

The supposed row is more complicated. Although it is conspicuous, an excavation would be required to confirm its validity as a man-made feature. Although the fallen stones appear to have been arranged, they may also be natural. Indeed, the row of stones points south-east, towards the winter solstice sunrise. For a culture that often made the effort to align their monuments towards the solstice sun, a natural row of stones would have made a perfect place to build an impressive burial mound.

Author's note: If we were to speculate, we could imagine there being a form of ritual gambling involved. Waking early on a frosty winter solstice morning, a farming community would congregate at the north end of the row. If blessed, the community would witness a sunrise, appearing from behind the barrow. This could indicate a good year, a reason to celebrate and thank the ancestors for their good fortune. If the conditions were not right, and the sun failed to emerge from the darkness, the community could expect a bleak winter ahead.

LOW BRIDESTONES

NZ 84575 04869

As you will learn from reading this book, stone rows are common in the North York Moors. In fact, outside Cornwall, Yorkshire has the highest concentration of stone rows in England. The Low Bridestones, which lay at the northern brow of Sleights Moor, may be either a prominent example of such a row or, as some have argued, a natural jumble of boulders.

A line of sixty stones, aligned over 65m, weaves its way east to west along the moor. Several of the stones stand upright, appearing to have been erected by human hands. Otherwise, only a mess of boulders is discernible, many of which do not form a row. Several mutilated cairns make up a part of its length, further confusing the site. Famed archaeologist Jacquetta Hawks took issue with the supposed row. She stated in a 1954 guidebook: 'The Low Bridestones are natural formations, curious weathered blocks of sandstone.'

Other archaeologists, such as Frank Elgee, agreed, believing the Low Bridestones were not part of a Bronze Age stone row. However, like many, Elgee believed they were erected by prehistoric people. He wrote in his 1930 *Early Man in North-east Yorkshire*: 'They undoubtedly represent the remains of stone-walled enclosures.' This idea remains the go-to theory when discussing the Low Bridestones.

Nevertheless, based on comparison alone, Early Bronze Age stone rows remain the most comparable moorland features. Stone rows had many different uses. Some rows were ceremonial monuments, aligned with the solstice sun. These were designed to accommodate gatherings. Other rows do not align with anything at all. Examples, such as North Ings Row, likely followed boundary lines, which were later fortified with mid-Bronze Age dykes. The Low Bridestones, although not a literal wall, may have represented a division in the landscape. Essentially, this may be an esoteric boundary, a kind of spiritual wall. As there are dozens of burial mounds on Sleights Moor, one could suggest the row demarcated the edge of a necropolis or ritual space.

RAMSDALE STONES & FYLINGDALES

NZ 92059 03776

Three standing stones poke above the foliage overlooking Robin Hood's Bay, on the aptly named Standing Stones Rigg. They stand on the northern edge of Fylingdales Moor, a U-shaped stretch of moorland home to several impressive monuments. To venture to the stones requires only a short walk from the A171 to the west.

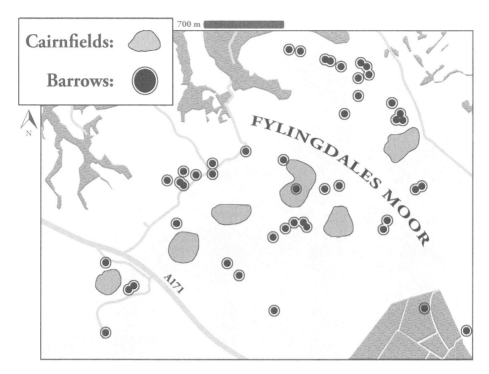

A MAP OF FYLINGDALES MOOR AND ITS MANY CAIRN-FIELDS.

The Ramsdale Stones are among the moor's better-understood landmarks. They stand in a triangular arrangement, with a space to the north-east shy of a missing stone. It would seem four stones once stood here, forming a square arrangement. Due to this, many sources use the term 'four-poster circle' to describe the Ramsdale Stones. Canmore, the Scottish record for the historic environment, describes four-poster circles as a 'setting of four upright stones'. These circles are most common in northern Britain and Scotland, especially along the east coast. However, in most cases these monuments turn out to be little more than damaged burial monuments, and therefore the term 'four-poster' is often a misnomer.

There are several theories about the purpose of these stones. It is possible that they were the inner chamber stones of a lost barrow. Indeed, the Robin Hood's Bay area is home to countless burial mounds, any number of which may cover hidden burial chambers. There are so many burial mounds above Robin Hood's Bay, photographing and individually describing them could fill an entire book alone.

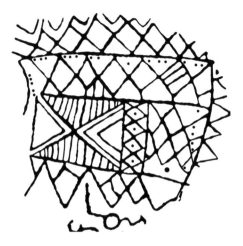

A SKETCH OF THE FIRE STONE MOTIF.

The largest collection survives on the adjacent Fylingdales Moor, where in 2003 a wildfire revealed over 150 previously unknown rock art sites. Moreover, locals walking the footpaths noticed newly revealed lumps in the landscape. Later surveys exposed a host of standing stones and burial cairns buried beneath the moor's surface. Archaeologist Blaise Vyner excavated one of these in 2005, revealing what was described as a 'unique small circular' monument. This arrangement of stones, which was more egg-like in shape, was placed around the perimeter of a pit. The purpose of such an enclosure remains unknown as excavations only covered a quarter of the circle's circumference.

Several of the uncovered kerb stones were arorned with intricate carvings on their inner sides. Unlike cup and ring marks, common in the North York Moors, these motifs were composed using straight lines, similar in style to mid to late Neolithic pottery and passage tomb art of western Britain. As the art was found on the inside of the kerb, and covered with a later cairn, it would suggest the art-bearing stones had been reused. This is best evidenced by the shape of the so-called 'Fire Stone', which had its art cropped by later reshaping.

BRECKON HOWE

NZ 85377 03407

Breckon Howe lies north-west of the A196, accessible via a footpath from a nearby cattle grid. It is one of many barrows on the moor, each with a Victorian cross adorning its top. A modern boundary stone juts from the top of Breckon Howe, distinguishing it from the rest. It is one of sixteen round barrows on Sleights Moor. Of these, Breckon Howe is the most prominent. Standing 2.1m tall and 19m in diameter, Breckon Howe lords over its surroundings from an elevated position. This position, below the moor's apex, is common among Bronze Age barrows. Building in such a position provides it with the illusion of scale, contrasting its silhouette against the distant sky.

With such bravado put into its design, we can infer a degree of one-upman-ship is taking place among burials in the area. The massive size of the mound and its commanding position allow it to dominate its surrounding land-scape. Breckon Howe is likely an early barrow that contained the bodies of many people in a style consistent with the Early Bronze Age. As this is one of many barrows on Sleights Moor, we can also assume it was used as a necropolis over several centuries.

Author's note: Over the road, to the east, there is a vast Bronze Age tumulus field, comprised of smaller burials. This is a fantastic place to see a cist, a stone coffin-like box created to hold bodies within burial mounds. The greatest mound is Greenland's Howe, at the edge of the moor (NZ 86879 03552), where an open cist is visible within an adjacent ruinous kerb.

SALTERGATE MOOR STONE ROW

SE 86487 95746

A row of three small sandstone boulders lies south of the Fylingdales RAF base. They are found 500m from the nearest footpath at the centre of Saltergate Moor and can be hard to see when the grass is tall. This is not the most awe-inspiring monument in Yorkshire, and as of 2022, there has been no conclusive proof that this is a prehistoric monument at all.

Stone rows often demarcate important Bronze Age landscapes, some ritual, others domestic or agricultural. In this case, the stones lay at the north-eastern edge of a cairn-field, where dozens of roughly built cairns were piled into groups. These 'clearance cairns' are the product of agricultural landscaping, piles of stones removed to form pastures. The pattern of clearance cairns suggests people were farming on this hillside during the Bronze Age.

The supposed row aligns to the south-west, towards the cairn-field. This would also orient the row towards the winter solstice sunset. Such a row, aligned towards both Bronze Age cairns and the solstice sun, may have held ritual importance. However, as they sit within a cairn-field, it may also be argued that these stones were dumped here along with the cairns during field clearance, marking a land boundary. These may simply represent an opportunistic use of megaliths during field clearance.

Author's note: Like many smaller stone rows, without context, we cannot be certain whether they served a ritual function or simply delineated practical boundaries. If this were a boundary formed with stones from adjacent field clearances, it would suggest the row marked a ritual boundary. Such opportunistic placements of megaliths still occur in the modern day, to enforce boundaries along roads or fields – easy to pass, but culturally understood as firm boundaries. But while today we use machinery to dump boulders in place as needed, in the Bronze Age, moving megaliths would have required a lot more effort. As such, prehistoric megaliths would possibly have evoked more admiration for the communities that erected them.

NEWGATE FOOT STONES (BLAKEY TOPPING)

SE 87191 93380

The Newgate Foot Stones sit on the southern edge of a plateau beneath Blakey Topping, east of the Hole of Horcum. Despite their significance, the stones are in a ruinous state, and their age and purpose remain unknown. Four standing stones survive at the site, each exhibiting signs of sculpting

THE LARGEST OF THE NEWGATE STANDING STONES.

and shaping. These stand in a rectangular formation. The northern corner lies on the eastern boundary of the adjacent field.

The stones are often referred to as a 'four-poster circle', like the Ramsdale Stones. Four-poster circles are typically small in diameter and are the remains of damaged burial mounds. However, no such mound appears to have been present on Newgate Foot. Instead, it has been argued that the stones are instead the remains of a larger stone circle. We may anticipate the remnants of a circle forming a rectangle if only the north and south ends survive. Given the site's proximity to the field's entrance, stone loss may have occurred along its western and eastern edges. Analysing the trajectory of the surviving portions of the site, one may imagine a circle around 20m in diameter. By Yorkshire standards, that is a very wide circle.

Others have put forth alternate theories. Historic England's scheduling article, for example, suggests it may be a damaged 'stone avenue'. Avenues comprise two stone rows running parallel through the landscape, forming a processional aisle. Such monuments often date to the early Bronze Age and are often found alongside stone circles. Often, stone avenues align towards the solstice sun, to the south-east or south-west. Yet these stones align north to south. If not the solstices, avenues may connect funerary monuments or stone circles. However, funerary monuments and stone circles are not found at Newgate Foot.

Of note are a cluster of over eighty cairns known as the **Thompson's Rigg Group**. These sit 1.3km south-east. The cairns are small and likely represent field clearances from Bronze and Iron Age settlement. Several of the larger cairns in the group appear to be burial monuments, arranged into a south-east alignment. The largest of these is 12m in diameter, which is below average for round cairns in the North York Moors.

HARWOOD DALE CIRCLE

SE 98241 96983

While many megalithic monuments take on an almost iconic role, serving as landmarks, rest stops and tourist traps, others lie unnoticed in relative isolation. This is not indicative of their importance, or even their impressiveness, but may instead reflect their inaccessibility. Nowhere is this clearer than at Harwood Dale, where an extraordinary burial mound lays relatively unknown. This is because, despite its impressiveness, Harwood Dale Circle lays out of reach and out of sight, away from footpaths and in the shade of dense forests.

It is a flat-topped mound surrounded by a prominent kerb of sixteen stones, the surviving base of a damaged burial monument. Of the few comparable sites in the North York Moors, such as Simon Howe and Nab Ridge, Harwood Dale Circle remains the best preserved. Like those other circles, this example likely dates to the Early Bronze Age (est. 2500 BC).

Nineteenth-century antiquarians took interest in the circle, excavating and surveying its inner area. Many of these investigations were never published, but some, such as those by John Tissiman, in 1852, were comprehensive. Tissiman had excavated a mound a year previously, at Rudda Cottages, uncovering several 'ornate slab-stones'. At that time, Harwood Dale Circle looked the same as it does today, as looting had already ravaged the site by 1820. Tissiman, for instance, mentions that there were originally '24 stones' in the kerb.

HARWOOD DALE CIRCLE.

ROCK ART THAT ONCE ADORNED HARWOOD DALE STONE CIRCLE.

THE RAVEN HALL
ROCK ART, NOW IN
THE YORKSHIRE
MUSEUM GARDENS.

After Tissiman's excavation at Harwood Dale, two of its stones – each deco-rated with deep cup and ring motifs – were moved to Scarborough Museum. These were likely early to mid-Neolithic in origin (est. 3800–3000 BC), so their inclusion within an Early Bronze Age burial monument is curious. There is some debate on related sites, where earlier rock art is used within later burial mounds. Is the rock art later? Is the burial monument earlier? Did the builders reuse rocks with earlier carvings?

Author's note: Harwood Dale Circle was not always so lonely. The area was once home to several similar kerbed burial monuments. The so-called Cloughton Moor Stone Circle (TA 00380 95947) was a compa-rable site, 2km to the south-east. A row of three massive barrows (among the largest in the moors), known as the Three Howes (SE 96601 98030), can still be found in the forests to the north-west.

If you find yourself in York, you can see an excellent example of the rock art from this region in the Museum Gardens, on a stone next to the museum's sign (SE 59971 52096). It is believed this stone was brought here by a Mr Raines in 1895, for temporary display at the York Philosophical Society. Archaeologists Graeme Chappell and Paul Brown believe this example originates from a lost barrow just south of Raven Hall Hotel in Ravenscar. William Greenwell described the stones here in 1890, noting that the hotel was in possession of eight carved stones looted from a nearby burial mound.

THE NORTHERN MOORS

The Northern Moors, stretching from Roseberry Topping in the west to Scaling Dam Reservoir in the east, form a well-defined barrier in the northern quarter of the national park. Unlike their counterparts in the south, these moors lack long valleys, instead rising straight from the Esk Valley to the North Sea. Between Guisborough and Lealholm there is little of note beyond a few chocolate box villages; a barren landscape perfect for the preservation of archaeological sites.

This rugged landscape is adorned with a rich array of prehistoric monuments, many of which are early to mid-Bronze Age burial mounds, built on the ridgeline to stand silhouetted against the sky. But beyond these common remains lie several unusual sites, seldom found elsewhere in Britain. In fact, of all the locations described in this chapter, the Northern Moors are home to the most unique and unparalleled assortment of prehistoric monuments.

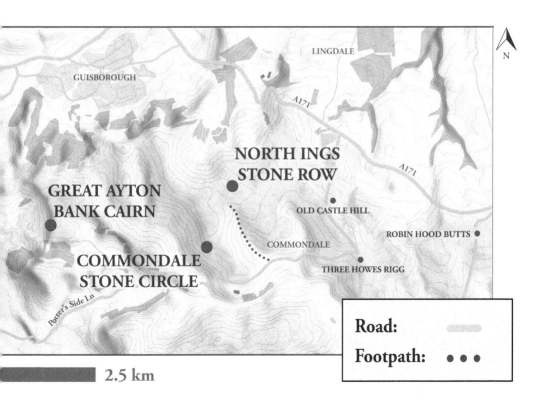

THE DANBY RIGG RING CAIRNS

NZ 70798 06573

A dense collection of prehistoric features survives on Danby Rigg, a moorland spur jutting out from Danby High Moor to the south. While there are many fascinating monuments here, most remain buried under the heather with little known about their form. For instance, the moor is home to the largest known collection of ring cairns in England, yet very few are visible from ground level.

The most obvious feature on the ridge is a 4ft-tall megalith (1.2m), standing next to the main footpath through the northern half of the moor. This nameless stone, which is believed to be a medieval way-marker, sits within a circular enclosure; a low rubble monument known as a ring cairn.

While stone circles are scarce in Yorkshire, ring cairns are abundant across the county's uplands. During the Early Bronze Age, people likely used ring cairns during funerals, as archaeologists frequently discover signs of cremation within them. They come in a variety of forms, which are often confused. The two most prominent variants are: embanked stone circles (where a small stone circle sits atop a ring cairn), and kerbed ring cairns (where the rubble bank is enclosed by a megalithic kerb).

THE STONE MARKING THE RING CAIRN CLOSEST TO THE FOOTPATH.

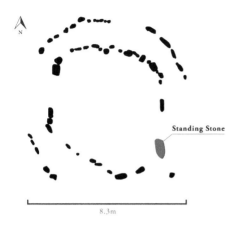

A PLAN OF DANBY RING CAIRN A.

Standing Stone

8.3m

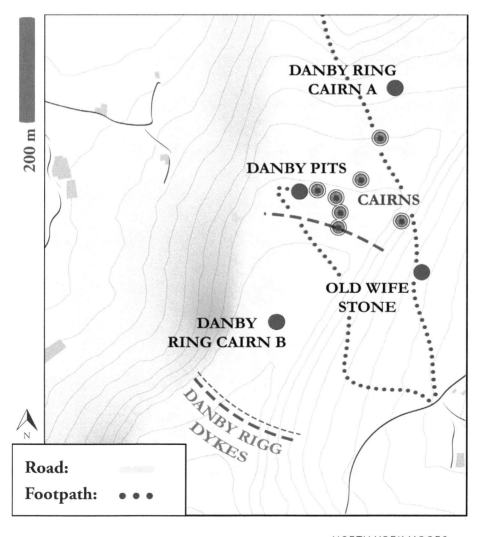

DANBY RING
CAIRN A

DANBY PITS

CAIRNS

OLD WIFE
STONE

DANBY
RING CAIRN B

DANBY RIGG
DYKES

200 m

N

Road:

Footpath: ● ● ●

DANBY RIGG (NZ 70670 06178)

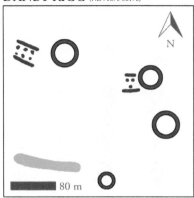

MIDDLE RIGG (NZ 73911 10784)

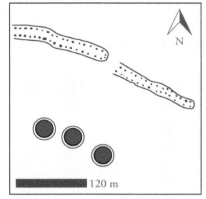

RING CAIRN: ⭘

ROUND CAIRN: ⬤

SEGMENTED PIT ENCLOSURE: ⠿

DANBY DYKE: —

WILKES MOOR (NZ 78148 09911)

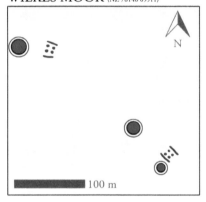

This ring cairn was excavated in the mid-nineteenth century by antiquarian J.C. Atkinson, and again in 2014 by Anthony Harding and Janusz Ostoja-Zagórski. The finds from these digs were typical of ring cairns in northern England, holding urns, flints and cremated remains. Like other ring cairns, it is likely that cremations were being carried out within the cairn's centre.

Author's note: As mentioned above, Danby Rigg is home to an unusually high number of ring cairns. There is no official tally, but I was able to spot at least nine. Why so many ring cairns were needed on this hill is not known, but it can be assumed the moor was a well-used necropolis during the Early Bronze Age. There are at least 800 cairns on the ridge, but it is unknown how many were built for burial purposes.

Scanning over an OS map, it is hard to miss the two large 'earthworks' spanning the width of the moor (at NZ 70773 06062). These comprise the Danby Rigg Dykes, two massive multi-ditched dykes, enclosing a 640m (2,000ft) area. While this was always believed to be a Bronze Age feature, the 2014 investigation of the moor revealed the dykes to be early medieval – possibly Viking. The implications of such a discovery are not limited to Danby Rigg. Indeed, one could argue that any number of undated dykes otherwise presumed to be Bronze Age may be early medieval (est. AD 800).

Several lesser features are visible south of the Danby Dyke. A standing stone, known as the **Old Wife Stone** (NZ 71039 05925), lies on the eastern slope of the moor (NZ 71038 05925). This was once one of a pair, aligned roughly east to west. Around the turn of the twentieth century, people removed the larger stone, leaving only the Old Wife Stone.

One of the more bizarre features on the moor lies just north of the Danby Dyke (NZ 70670 06179). This feature, which we will refer to as the Danby Rigg Pits, is a segmented earthwork, consisting of rows of pits enclosed between two parallel ditches. Although curious, it is not the only example of such a site in Yorkshire. Three such features exist; the other two surviving on Middle Rigg (NZ 73908 10784) and Wilkes Moor (NZ 78147 09912). One theory suggests these sites are not actually monuments but instead the incomplete remains of dykes. The largest example survives on Middle Rigg, north of Houlsyke, which forms an unusual boundary along the length of an Early Bronze Age barrow cemetery.

COMMONDALE STONE CIRCLE

NZ 63779 10855

Commondale Stone Circle, which is also called the Sleddale Stone Circle, stands at the centre of Wayworth Moor, located east of Sleddale Beck. To access the circle, it requires a 2km walk up a nearby gamekeeper's track to the south-east. Throughout the summer it can be difficult to see due to the heather cover.

This 38m-wide circle sits on a low slope, dominating the Leven Valley to the south. What appears to be a stone row snakes away from the circle's eastern edge, roughly aligned south-east to south-west. Stone circles of this size,

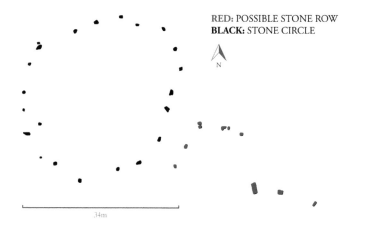

RED: POSSIBLE STONE ROW
BLACK: STONE CIRCLE

N

34m

A PLAN OF
COMMONDALE
STONE CIRCLE.

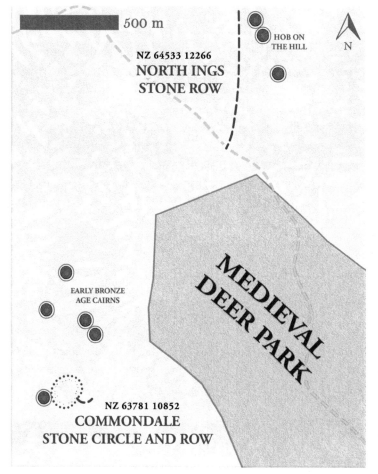

500 m

N

NZ 64533 12266
**NORTH INGS
STONE ROW**

HOB ON
THE HILL

**MEDIEVAL
DEER PARK**

EARLY BRONZE
AGE CAIRNS

NZ 63781 10852
**COMMONDALE
STONE CIRCLE AND ROW**

A MAP OF THE
LANDSCAPE
BETWEEN
NORTH INGS
AND THE
COMMONDALE
CIRCLE.

sometimes known as Cumbrian circles, are not known to exist in Yorkshire. As their name suggests, similar circles are far more abundant in north-west England, as well as in Cornwall, Ireland and Scotland, where people used megaliths to construct large ceremonial enclosures. Such circles often date to the mid to late Neolithic period (est. 3200–2500 BC).

In Yorkshire, stone circles wide enough to walk around inside typically sit on top of ring cairns, averaging between 15 and 20m in diameter, far smaller than this example. These monuments, known as embanked stone circles, dot Yorkshire's uplands, representing Early Bronze Age funerary activity (see Chapter 3, Ox Close Stone Circle). However, no trace of a ring cairn survives in this instance, and there is no evidence of any burial-related monuments within the circumference of the circle, leading to speculation that it may be an unusual monument, possibly even a Cumbrian circle.

If this is a Cumbrian circle, it likely enclosed many activities and had several uses. Given that many stone circles are aligned with the sun and moon, it is possible that the site was used as a calendar. There is also suggestion that Cumbrian circles had deep religious significance, as evidenced by burials and offerings found at some sites. Indeed, the purpose of stone circles may have been a combination of practical and religious factors.

One interesting connection is best observed from an aerial perspective. To the north, a stone row known as **North Ings** (see next entry), snakes its way north to south across the moor, before terminating beside the footpath. This path marks an important boundary, where a medieval deer park bounds the track in parallel, marked by a dyke. There is, therefore, the possibility that the southern span of North Ings Row was removed during the medieval period. Had North Ings continued past this point, it may have met the small row joining Commondale Stone Circle.

Sadly, many believe this is too good to be true. The circle, which only stands in a loose oval configuration, was first mentioned as late as 1930 in Frank Elgee's *Early Man in North East Yorkshire*. Upon visiting the site in the late 1950s, archaeologist Raymond H. Hayes believed the site to have been a modern creation, noting how several of the stones were loosely held in place. Later excavations conducted in the 1960s yielded limited results, consisting only of scattered quartz stones and some flints. To this day, no definitive evidence has been discovered to prove the authenticity of the circle.

NORTH INGS STONE ROW

NZ 64498 12019

Snaking roughly 500m north to south across North Ings Moor, this colossal stone row is both the longest and most striking example of such a monument in Yorkshire. Venturing to the site requires passing North Ings Farm via the farm track up Thunderbush Moor. The row and its adjacent earthwork terminate at the footpath.

It runs north over an upland spur, aligned east to west. Once crested, the spur allows unobstructed views over the Irish Sea to the north. The ridgeline marking these spectacular views is strewn with Early Bronze Age burial mounds. The two largest of these are **Hob on the Hill**, which sits east of North Ings Stone Row, and **Black Howes**, a kerbed mound visible to the far east.

Nineteenth-century antiquarians excavated both mounds, discovering burial goods from the Early Bronze Age. They found pottery and hairpins, as well as many later mid-Bronze Age burials. In 1863, the antiquarian J.S. Atkinson opened the primary cist inside Hob on the Hill. Inside, he found a small pot, along with several Bronze Age arrowheads. He uncovered an additional five later burials that had been inserted into the side of the mound, together with bone jewellery and flint tools.

Like other round barrows in the North York Moors, their position suggests domination over the landscape was important to those who ruled over Early Bronze Age Britain. They draw a line along the spur, from east to west, marking where lowland views are best observed. Smaller barrows are paired with both Black Howes and Hob on the Hill, aligning them towards the open vista to the north. This is an alignment shared with the stone row, which runs cross ridge, perpendicular to the ridgeline.

HOB ON THE HILL.

ABOVE: THE SOUTHERN END OF ROW. *BELOW:* THE CENTRAL SECTION OF THE ROW.

North Ing's Stone Row runs parallel to an adjacent cross-ridge dyke. An excavation in 1991 demonstrated that the row predated this dyke, which was either mid to late Bronze Age, Iron Age or early medieval in origin. The incorporation of early monuments into later defensive boundaries is seen repeatedly throughout the North York Moors, from standing stones to solstice-aligned burial mound cemeteries (see Cleave Dyke System). Like other cross-ridge dykes, the North Ings example was likely defensive.

While this may have been the case, the stone row is likely more than a simple boundary marker. If we are to place the row into an Early Bronze Age context, we must see it through its connection to the nearby barrows. Like the barrows, the stone row may have been guiding people towards the sea vistas to the north. Unlike the later dyke, which likely had its focus set on the east, working as a defensive earthwork, the stone row may have, like the barrows, been working to reinforce the natural splendour of the ridgeline.

CROWN END STONE ROW

NZ 66065 07112

You can find this stone row north of Westerdale, among the Crown End grouse butts. It can be reached via a footpath from Upper Esk Road, which cuts over the moor from Westerdale.

Despite its prominence in the landscape, little is known about the row. From the looks of things, it is something of a sister site to North Ings. Like North Ings, Crown End has a dyke running a portion of its northern length, and its stones are around the same height and weight. Its length is far shorter, as it would appear much of its southern half has been lost. The largest stone belongs to the row's southern end, which stands alone on the south side of the ridge.

The moor itself is a treasure trove of Early Bronze Age remains. To the east of the row is a well-preserved settlement, which was inhabited sporadically between the Early Bronze Age and Iron Age (est. 2000 BC–AD 43). The settlement is largely invisible from ground level, is fragile and is protected by law, so visitation is not recommended. Interestingly though, the stone row does appear to mark the spur of land the settlement sits on, and like at North Ings, it was later recut with the dyke. This may be an exceedingly rare example of a monument and its mother settlement surviving together in the landscape.

OLD CASTLE HILL STONE ROW (LOST)

NZ 67361 12016

The desolate scene that greets you at the Old Castle Hill Stone Row is a sad reminder of the frailty of UK archaeology. In its former glory, this Early Bronze Age stone row, positioned along a moorland ridge, was as grand as Crown End or North Ings. Archaeologist Frank Elgee visited and photographed the site in the early 1930s. At that time, at least five stones could be seen standing, but today only two fallen stones remain, both small and unremarkable.

OLD CASTLE HILL'S WESTERNMOST STONE.

GREAT AYTON BANK CAIRN AND PASSAGE TOMB

NZ 59377 11488

Great Ayton Moor is best known for its views over Roseberry Topping, a steep-sided hill overlooking the village of Great Ayton. But, for those interested in archaeology, there is a far better reason to visit. On a spur of land, poking up from the southern corner of the moor, you can find one of the most remarkable collections of prehistoric monuments in England.

The clearest feature here is an Iron Age enclosure (est. 200 BC). It is 50m in diameter and square in form, with an entrance facing eastwards. This entrance leads out onto an ancient trackway, which continues straight down the moor to the valley bottom. Two stone and earth banks, separated by a broad ditch, define the enclosure. This is not a monument, but rather a defensive homestead of some variety, comparable to a hill fort. During the 1950s, archaeologists excavated the site, uncovering Iron Age pottery and the foundations of several huts.

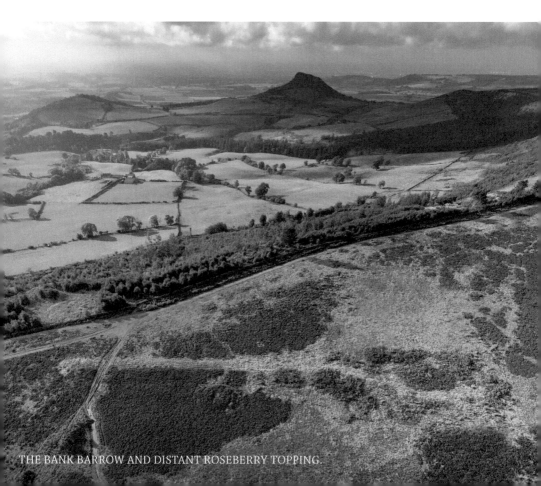

THE BANK BARROW AND DISTANT ROSEBERRY TOPPING.

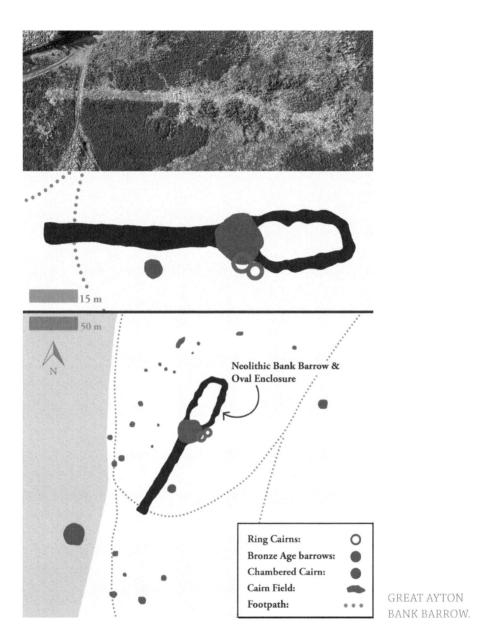

Ring Cairns: ○
Bronze Age barrows: ●
Chambered Cairn: ●
Cairn Field: ◣
Footpath: • • •

Neolithic Bank Barrow & Oval Enclosure

15 m
50 m
N

GREAT AYTON BANK BARROW.

All around this enclosure, especially in the heather to the north-west, are small cairns. These are clearance piles, moved here to make way for agricultural activity during the mid to late Bronze Age (est. 1800–700 BC). These become more numerous the further west you head, towards the treeline at the brow of the moor. Among this clearance are several earlier burial cairns, dating to the Early Bronze Age (est. 2500 BC).

Within this dense, multi-period cairn-field, you can find the most fascinating landmarks on the moor. On a south-facing slope overlooking Hunter's Scar are two rare Neolithic monuments: a **passage tomb**, and a **bank cairn**. These features are part of a single spoon-shaped megastructure, aligned south-west to north-east.

There is nothing remarkable to see at ground level. No lumps, bumps or stones. The only shadows cast are by the few scattered pine trees to the west. Although bracken grows densely around the cairn, the level ground that stretches along the length of the structure remains unobstructed and visible to the naked eye. This creates a grand display of clarity amidst the heather.

Bank cairns are among Britain's rarest monuments, dating to the early Neolithic period (est. 3500 BC). They are most often found in southern England, especially to the west. Researchers have measured examples in Cornwall that are around 400m (a quarter of a mile) in length, far surpassing the length of other burial monuments in Britain. It remains a mystery why early Neolithic people built such a monument, characteristic of south-west England, on Great Ayton Moor. Its isolated position may be an example of cultural diversity during the early Neolithic, as groups met, traded and influenced each other over considerable distances.

The bank cairn on Great Ayton Moor is 120m (400ft) long, with a squared-off terminal at its southern end. Its northern end terminates in a bizarre oval enclosure. Whether the two constitute a single structure is not known, as the passage tomb sits between them, covering the point where they would have met. Two pitted mounds sit within the oval enclosure, which may have been graves. If so, it seems someone robbed them a long time ago. There are also three small cairns built into the sides of the enclosure, which may be part of the surrounding cairn-field.

The passage tomb at the centre of the monument is often described as a chambered cairn. Any tomb containing chambers may be called chambered, yet only those with a long passage leading into said chambers may be called passage tombs. Such monuments are rare in Britain, tending to hold the grandest of mid to late Neolithic burials (est. 3200 BC). However, as most large cairns in England remain unexcavated, it is not clear how many may contain inner passages or chambers. As such, most chambered tombs and passage tombs in England may remain unidentified.

THE PASSAGE TOMB'S END CHAMBER.

S.V. Morris led excavations at the site in 1953, and R.H. Hayes continued the work from then until 1960. The most apparent element of the cairn discovered was a rectangular chamber 4m in length. The builders constructed this chamber using megalithic stones, capping it off with a 2m (7ft)-wide end slab. They then built a 2m-long passage to reach the chamber, which was aligned in a north-west to south-east direction. Curiously, it appears the chamber had been left open for some time, and a firepit had been dug into the floor of the chamber.

Typically, archaeologists find disarticulated bones within Neolithic burial chambers, but here no bones were ever found. Nevertheless, evidence of bone removal shortly after burial has been found in comparable Neolithic chambered tombs. In rare instances, people even fashioned these bones into jewellery. Often, after some time spent removing and reinterring the bones of the dead, the passage and chamber were filled in and the site decommissioned. This practice seems to have occurred here, as the passage and empty chamber were filled with rubble, and later covered with a cairn.

The final additions to the site were several round cairns, off alignment with the bank cairn, and two ring cairns that were built into the eastern side of the passage tomb. The 1953 excavation revealed that people used these monuments during cremations. Inside the northernmost ring cairn, a cist was found, covering several urns. Additionally, during this period (est. 2500–1800 BC) many later burials were inserted into the side of the passage tomb.

SISS CROSS HILL / DIMMINGDALE ENCLOSURES

NZ 69999 11063/NZ 68588 11877

While the oval enclosure on the northern end of the Great Ayton Bank Cairn is unusual, 9km (6 miles) to the east, two similar enclosures survive on Danby Low Moor. They are difficult to see from ground level, and other than several Bronze Age cairns, little else survives in their surrounding area. The example on Siss Cross Hill sits in the middle of an alignment of four Bronze Age round barrows.

It has been posited that the two enclosures are mid-Bronze Age in origin, as a 1952 excavation uncovered a cremation pit from that era. R.H. Hayes, who organised the excavation, believed they were enclosed urn fields, the mid to

ONE OF THE BARROWS NEAR THE ENCLOSURE, KNOWN AS ROBIN HOOD'S BUTTS.

late Bronze Age equivalent of a cemetery. However, given their similar appearance to the Great Ayton example, there is a chance the enclosures are Neolithic in origin. Interestingly, it seems this style of enclosure was wholly unique to the northernmost moors of Yorkshire.

Author's note: You can find a similar northern English bank cairn in better condition near the Scottish border, at a site known as Bellshiel Law (NT 81329 01173).

THE HAMBLETON HILLS

The Hambleton Hills span 20km, from Swainby in the north down to Kilburn, marked by England's largest hill figure, the White Horse. The majority of surviving prehistoric features on these hills are burial mounds. However, three landmark monuments survive on the hills, demonstrating a continuity of use from the early Neolithic through the mid to late Bronze Age (3600–700 BC).

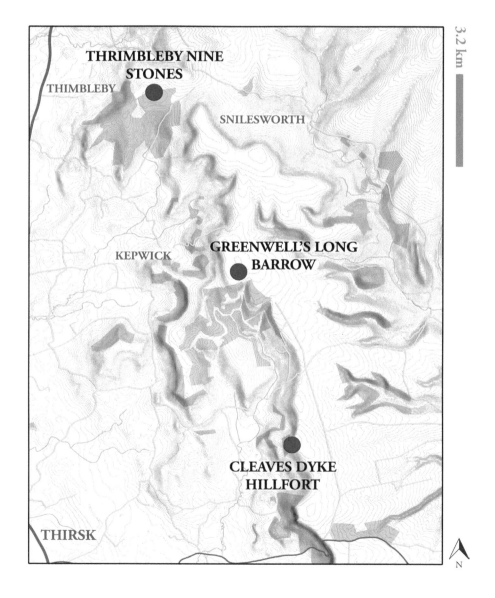

The Cleveland Way, a footpath spanning 175km (110 miles), courses its path past all three sites detailed in this section. The trail was opened to the public in 1969, becoming the second National Trail recognised by the UK government. The product of years of pressure from the Teesside Ramblers Association, the initial idea for the trail was to link the east coast to the Cleveland Hills. The resultant long-distance walk encompasses more, leading anticlockwise around almost the entire circumference of the moors.

More than a simple coincidence, the co-occupation of this modern footpath and prehistoric monuments makes perfect sense. Just as the western edge of the Cleveland Way was designed to allow views over the Vale of Mowbray, so too were the many Bronze Age burial monuments that dot the hills. As the footpath marks a route of least resistance across the edge of the hillside, it may be assumed that prehistoric people also ventured down a similar pathway.

GREENWELL'S LONG BARROW

SE 49156 90337

Greenwell's Long Barrow, also known as the Kepwick Long Barrow, is a little-known archaeological gem. It is low lying and nestled among dense fields of moorland bracken, making it hard to see in the warmer months. It lies in a field west of the Cleveland Way path.

GREENWELL'S LONG BARROW LOOKING WEST.

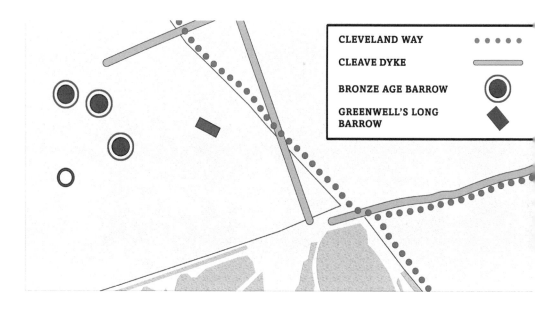

This unassuming mound represents Britain's oldest monumental burial tradition. Dating between 3700 BC and 3200 BC, long barrows are the best-known monuments of the early Neolithic period. In typical Neolithic fashion, long barrows were shared spaces for the dead; communal tombs where the bones of many people were interred. These were likely people who held sway in their communities, either political or religious leaders. Recent genetic studies have revealed that bodies interred in long barrows were often related. This may suggest they were used dynastically – not unlike Westminster Cathedral or the tombs of ancient Egypt.

While not the grandest example of such a monument, Greenwell's Long Barrow survives well. It stands over 1m high (4ft), and spans 30m in length (100ft). It was oriented towards the south-east, aligned to the winter solstice sunrise. Like most long barrows, it has the shape of a door wedge, broadening towards the east, sloping up from one end to the other.

William Greenwell (the barrow's namesake), best known for his work at Grime's Graves in Norfolk, excavated the long barrow in the nineteenth century. Along the spine of the barrow, several collections of bones were discovered. It is likely that these skeletons were 'excarnated' before they were buried, meaning that their flesh and organs were removed. As such, they had been inserted into the long barrow as loose skeletons – at least five individuals. He found no burial goods.

Nearby, there are three large round barrows and a ring cairn. These mounds, which date to the Early Bronze Age, might be up to a thousand years younger than the long barrow. To the immediate east, is the Cleave Dyke System, an immense mid-Bronze Age earthwork (see next entry). These later monuments represent a clear land division, stretching from north to south along the natural slope of the moor. Curiously, Greenwell's Long Barrow has survived well, despite the intense Bronze Age activity nearby. It would seem respect for the site lingered well into the Bronze Age, becoming part of a larger land boundary.

CLEAVE DYKE SYSTEM/BOLTBY SCAR

SE 50628 85653

The Cleave Dyke System, which runs from Kepwick to Hambleton, is one of Yorkshire's largest prehistoric earthworks. Following the contours of Hambleton Down, a flat-topped hill overlooking Thirsk, Cleave Dyke roughly aligns with the Cleveland Way. This is one of the youngest sites listed in this book, dating to the mid to late Bronze Age. We will be focusing on the small stretch at Boltby Scar, between Cleveland Road to the west, and Boltby to the east.

THE BARROW ON SUTTON BANK, AS SEEN FROM BOLTBY SCAR.

Over 8km of earthworks snake their way through the landscape. These linear ditches, often several metres deep, form square divisions in the land over many kilometres. These are thought to be land boundaries, which are not to be confused with field systems. Dykes were not always practical as field boundaries, and they instead seem to have served as grandiose displays of land ownership.

On first inspection, it would seem the dyke provided a boundary facing west, defending the eastern hillside. However, not only would this be impractical, but earlier archaeology may contradict this. An incredible thirty-eight round burial mounds run parallel to the dyke, predating it by at least 800 years. In typical Bronze Age fashion, the mounds stand proud along the cliff side of Hambleton Down. There is also evidence, in the form of crop marks, of a stone or timber row running parallel to the mounds. This also predates the dyke and may be as old as the Middle Neolithic period (3200 BC). Additionally, archaeologists have discovered early Neolithic tools and pottery in the vicinity of Boltby Scar. Among these was a polished stone axe believed to have originated from the Langdale Valley in the Lake District.

A SECTION OF CLEAVE DYKE NEAR GREENWELL'S LONG BARROW.

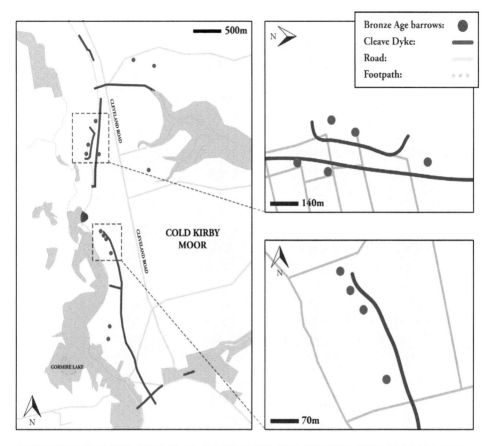

A MAP SHOWING THE COURSE OF CLEAVE DYKE AND ITS SURROUNDING BARROWS.

This little spur of land was evidently occupied for a long stretch of time. But what does this suggest? For one thing, the linear path of the barrows implies the boundary was well established for centuries. It appears as if the dyke surrounded this earlier necropolis of barrows, as most of the barrows are sandwiched between the cliff face and the dyke. If the barrows were regarded as important in a religious sense, it may have been appropriate to protect them in this way.

Around 400 BC, people of the Iron Age integrated several forts into the dyke system. On Boltby Scar, you can find a small promontory fort, where a single dyke and wall once sealed off and defended the hillside, while on Roulston Scar, beside the White Horse, one of northern England's largest hill forts was rediscovered in the year 2000. It is possible that the Cleave Dyke System was reused in the Iron Age, with defensive outposts dotting its length.

NINE STONES ROW

SE 47078 95310

Nine Stones Row sits at the centre of Thimbleby Moor, 1km west of the Cleveland Way. To see it requires a boggy walk, heading off-footpath over dense heather. The easiest approach is to follow the footpath west from Square Corner, before veering off south. Follow the grouse butts towards the treeline. You want to then head east and aim for the brow of the moor. Two standing stones will greet you, and you will see an additional two by the wall to the south.

The stones sit in two collections, supposedly forming a double row spanning 60m, aligned north to south. Not quite parallel to one another, they converge at their northern end. There is a gap in the row's centre, splitting it into two groupings: one north and one south. There is little doubt these are prehistoric standing stones; that much is evident in their weathering. Yet, the site has some interesting quirks.

This type of north-to-south aligned double row is unusual. Of the thirteen similar stone rows in Britain, only two others, both found in Cornwall, align north to south. Of the three, only the Nine Stones Row does not end in a burial cairn. Indeed, we may argue that the stones may not be the remains of a row at all, but rather two distinct monuments. We may be looking at the kerbstones of two lost burial mounds.

THE NORTHERN PORTION OF THE SUPPOSED ROW.

SCARTH WOOD MOOR CEMETERY/
NEAR MOOR ROCK ART

SE 46856 99959

A well-preserved collection of six burial mounds lies north of Cod Beck Reservoir, south of the Cleveland Way. They are labelled A to F and have all been looted. The best preserved is Barrow E (SE 46854 9958), which has a bank and ditch surrounding it. Most burial mounds in northern England have lost their outer ditch and bank, so this is rare.

To the immediate west, on Near Moor, you can find a multitude of rock art panels. So far, twenty-five rocks featuring motifs have been identified on the moor, but it is likely more are hidden underneath the heather.

The motifs, cups arranged in parallel lines, are characteristic of the Neolithic period. Such motifs are rare in the North York Moors, where they are more often paired with ring marks. Some argue cup marks like these, found on natural crags, predate ring markings by a matter of centuries, originating in the Early Neolithic.

HOWE HILL

SE 46738 84623

For much of the twentieth century, Howe Hill, a large mound at the centre of Felixkirk, was believed to be the remains of a medieval motte-and-bailey castle. However, like several sites in the Vale of Mowbray, it is now believed to be a natural hill topped with a burial mound, possibly of Neolithic origin. Incidentally, the place name 'Howe' means tumulus, so Howe Hill literally translates as 'Tumulus Hill'.

OTHER SITES IN THE NORTH YORK MOORS

NEWTON MULGRAVE LONG BARROW/
STANG HOWE

NZ 77613 14327

There is a collection of at least eight prehistoric burial mounds on Newton Mulgrave Moor. The majority of these are Early Bronze Age round barrows. The largest mound is known as Stang Howe, which lies to the far west of the moor, near Cliff Brow Road. The archaeological consensus is that Stang Howe is a natural knoll that was considered important regardless. Early Bronze Age builders may have mistaken it for a Neolithic burial mound, revering it as an ancestral feature.

Additionally, an Early Neolithic long barrow sits at the north-eastern corner of the moor. It has been mutilated, and appears broader than it would have originally been, its top having slid down into its external ditches. It is similar to Greenwell's Long Barrow in the Hambleton Hills. The two sites represent a regional variant of the long barrow, small and trapezoidal with two flanking ditches on each broad side.

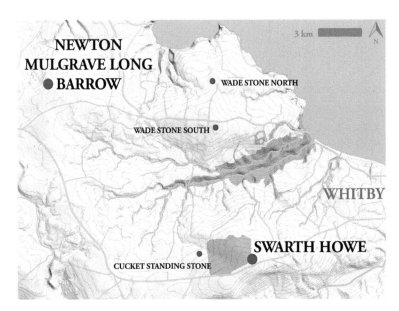

THE MANY MONUMENTS WEST OF WHITBY.

THE CUCKET STONE

NZ 82509 09056

One of several standing stones in the area north of the Moors, including the Wades Stones and Swarth Howe. It stands within a private field home to many Bronze Age remains, including two round cairns and a visible field system. The stone itself is likely the remains of a ruined cist, possibly a capstone.

THE WADES STONES

NZ 82953 14414/NZ 83050 13009

These two blocky standing stones are found to the south of Kettleness, in private fields either side of the A174. They were both once part of a pair but only a single stone survives at each site. At the base of the southern stone, an Anglo-Saxon (est. AD 600) cremated burial and spearhead were found; these were likely later in date than the stone.

RABBIT HILL BARROW

SE 41417 96865

East of Northallerton, in the fields opposite the hamlet of Winton, you may notice a curious lump. This is the mutilated remains of a lonely round barrow. It has had its sides sheared off by ploughing, making it square in form. It originally had a surrounding ditch, but this has long since eroded away. Whether the barrow was ever excavated is not known, but it seems to have remained well preserved.

THE RABBIT HILL BARROW.

CAMMON STONE / THREE HOWES

SE 62676 99997

One of the North York Moors' best standing stones, the Cammon Stone stands on Cockayne Ridge. Access is simple, but requires either a long walk along the ridge or a climb up from Cockayne. It was allegedly once one of several standing stones on the ridge, and nineteenth-century maps mark several lost archaeological features. Chance finds on the moor have revealed the ridge was occupied throughout prehistory. Tools and arrowheads have been discovered poking up from the earth, and clearance cairns can be seen when the heather is burned.

There are also several round barrows surviving on the ridge. Some of these, such as **Cold Moor Round Barrow**, have prominent kerb stones surrounding them, much like the Nab Ridge Bride Stones. The most-visited collection is known as the Three Howes, but there are at least six barrows on the hillside.

THE BLACKPARK STONE

SE 75250 90932

Since the nineteenth century, there have been dozens of prehistoric artefacts and monuments unearthed in the forests north of Cropton. Within their dark recesses, you can find sections of a cross dyke, and at least two bowl barrows. Early to mid-Bronze Age activity seems to have been prevalent here, as chance finds have unearthed both a large urn and an incense cup (a smaller vessel placed beside a burial). In the 1930s, a Neolithic polished axe head was unearthed, suggesting Neolithic activity. As a result of all this activity, a stone at the far south of the forest may be of Neolithic origin.

Known as the **Blackpark Stone**, it stands in a clearing of trees 135m up the track towards the nearby holiday park. Throughout much of the year, it is shrouded in bracken. However, during the winter, the 5ft-tall stone can be spotted from the road. Some consider it to be associated with the nearby dyke, while others are unsure of its legitimacy as a prehistoric feature all together. Not all stones that stand are standing stones, and very few of them are proven to be prehistoric in date.

SWARTH HOWE STONE ROW

NZ 84209 08931

In Hutton Mulgrave Wood, just north of the A171, there is a row of stones trailing off from a large round cairn. On the surface, the cairn is far more prominent than the row, which disappears into the nearby forest, making it hard to see throughout the warmer months. Had the site not been overgrown, it may have resembled the stone rows of the Goathland area, such as Simon Howe and the High Bridestones.

NORTH RIDING FOREST PARK

There is a vast complex of burial mounds in the North Riding Forest Park, south of the Blakey Raise Standing Stones – far too many to cover in this book. Over 100 round barrows and cairns have been preserved in the forests. The majority of these are Bronze Age, but there are some rare Iron Age square barrows hidden among them. The dense forests and private land make visiting the mounds difficult.

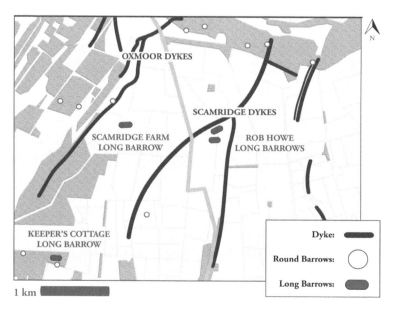

THE LONG BARROWS AND DYKES SOUTH OF NORTH RIDING FOREST PARK.

The easiest barrows to visit are **Fox Howes**, **Three Howes** and **Brown Howes** (see the back of this book for grid references). These are found just off Dalby Forest Road, skirting the eastern edge of the forest park. Near these barrows is a system of dykes, so vast in scale that photography could not do justice. The largest of these are the Oxmoor and Scamridge Dykes, which snake several kilometres south of the forests. Although they date to the mid-Bronze Age (est. 1000–700 BC), the dykes appear to follow the alignments of several Early Neolithic long barrows (est. 3500 BC). The best preserved of these is the **Scamridge Farm Long Barrow**, which lies deep in private land and has no nearby footpaths. Such earthworks are more common in the south, in the Wolds. As these are less than 10km from the Wolds, they may be connected.

HARLAND MOOR STONE CIRCLE

SE 67527 92610

Situated away from the most prominent prehistoric landscapes in the moors, Harland Moor is impressive in its banality. There are many small cairns on the moor and its surrounding landscape. The majority of these represent field clearance, having been heaped out of the way of farmland pasture in the Bronze and Iron Ages. But remarkably, there is also what appears to be an Early Bronze Age stone circle. The circle is situated on the side of the moor close to Daleside Road, which snakes its way past Gillamoor and Low Mill.

Due to its sorry state of preservation, there is little to see on the ground surface. Some believe it to be the remaining kerb from a destroyed burial cairn, while others believe it to be nothing more than the remains of a modern sheep fold. However, the stones do appear to sit on a small embankment, which may be a ring cairn. Such layered circles, variously known as embanked stone circles, cremation cemeteries and sometimes ring cairns, are common across northern England. Excavations in Cumbria and Lancashire have demonstrated that

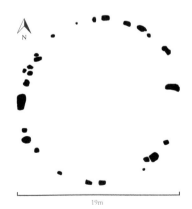

HARLAND MOOR STONE CIRCLE.

many generations would use such enclosures to perform funerals. While this example is not ideal for demonstration purposes, there are several more embanked circles detailed in Chapter 3.

STUDFOLD RING

SE 58128 79864

The Studfold Ring, a massive earthwork enclosure north of the village of Ampleforth, is something of an enigma. The eponymous 'ring' is a square embankment surrounding an inner trench, with a single entrance and rounded corners. The peculiar shape of the enclosure, with its inner trench and outer embankment, has led some to believe it is a converted Neolithic henge, reshaped to serve as a stud (horse) fold (enclosed pasture) during the medieval period. However, besides its unique appearance, little concrete evidence points in any definitive direction.

Several burial mounds were once located around the earthwork, many of which were excavated and removed in the mid-nineteenth century. Antiquarian Georgy Frank wrote of one of these barrows in 1888, noting: 'A third, opened ... as long ago as 1808, was formed of a large circle of massive stones with an urn in the centre.' Further excavations occurred in 1966, revealing pottery under the barrows. These excavations, as well as radiocarbon dating results, suggest the field was used throughout prehistory, and confirm that ritual activity was occurring around Studfold Ring during the Neolithic.Could this be a Neolithic henge hidden in plain sight?

ROSEBERRY STONE

NZ 57032 13054

An unnamed standing stone, which we shall label the Roseberry Stone, sits in the village green of Newton under Roseberry. Little is known about its origins, but some have argued that it is the lone survivor of a lost stone row. There is little evidence of this, and its situation suggests otherwise. In a field north of the green is a large rectangular earthwork, which may be an enclosure like those at Great Ayton and Siss Hill.

THE ROSEBERRY STONE.

ALLAN TOFTS ROCK ART

NZ 83000 03000

There is a dense collection of rock art on Allan Tofts Moor, just north of Goathland. The motifs are highly weathered, having been beaten down by millennia of rain. The carvings that remain visible, which are best seen burnished after light rain, are similar to those at the Wainstones.

BOG HOUSE STONE

SE 65508 93297

This 1.3m-high stone sits in a marshy field east of Bog House Farm. Its location is uninspiring, sitting back, away from views over Bransdale. Ordinance Survey marks the site as 'standing stones', believing the stone to have been one of a prehistoric pair. Others believe the stone to have been erected to mark the location of a spring in the medieval period.

HELMSLEY BARROWS

SE 62191 83768

Just east of the village of Helmsley, on the very cusp of the North York Moors, you can find a collection of three Early Bronze Age round barrows. These are the last survivors of an original nine in the area. Six were removed via excavation in the nineteenth century, finding Early Bronze Age and Neolithic artefacts. This included a polished stone axe, as well as several urns. There is the possibility that at least one of these mounds was of Early Neolithic origin (est. 3400 BC).

CHAPTER TWO

THE VALES OF MOWBRAY AND YORK, THE HEART OF NEOLITHIC YORKSHIRE

In this small chapter we will focus on the largest and arguably most impressive prehistoric landscape in Yorkshire. Here, within the fertile Vales of Mowbray and York, where the Tees winds its way to the north and the Ouse to the south, you can still hear the heartbeat of long-dead cultures. While this wide valley covers vast swathes of Yorkshire between the Moors and the Dales, we will be focusing on only a small section, between Leeming Bar and Boroughbridge, a landscape we will refer to as 'the Heart of Neolithic Yorkshire'. It was on this tract of land, over 5,000 years ago, that Neolithic people chose to construct one of Britain's largest ritual landscapes.

The A1(M), Yorkshire's largest motorway, crosses through the centre of this sweeping valley. Prehistoric tracks, much like modern motorways, may have followed this route of least resistance. With Scotland to the north, the Thames to the south, the Lake District to the west and the coast to the east, this would have been an attractive area to settle for trade. Moreover, large rivers, like the Ure and Swale, would have enabled Neolithic people to traverse through the wooded landscapes of the time.

A prehistoric 'survivor's bias' is clear across Britain. By this, we mean that archaeological sites positioned in the most habitable areas have been largely lost to time – swallowed up by towns and cities. Therefore, research in areas of high human activity demonstrates a bias towards only the largest and

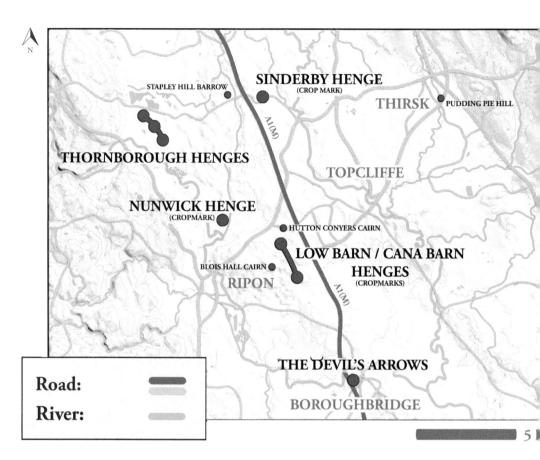

Road:

River:

hardiest surviving examples. There are a few sites so magnificent that even in the most developed areas they have remained unwavering in the face of encroaching urbanism. Among such monuments are Stonehenge and Avebury in Wiltshire, Mayburgh Henge in Cumbria and Newgrange in County Meath. You would expect such landscapes, so close to modern settlements, to have been swallowed by the ravages of time. But their sheer scale and impressiveness have helped secure their survival.

The Vales of Mowbray and York are **not** examples of such places. Much of the archaeology in the valley has been lost to time. We have only come to discover the immensity of the region's archaeology in recent years, as aerial photography has revealed dozens of massive monuments across the region. As such, unlike Stonehenge, Mayburgh or Newgrange, the grandeur of the Heart of Neolithic Yorkshire never rose to the iconic ranks of its peers.

THE THORNBOROUGH HENGES

SE 28522 79462

A small tract of land between Thornborough, a village north of Ripon, and the River Ure, contains an incredible collection of Neolithic earthworks. So impressive is this region, it is often awarded the trite moniker 'the Stonehenge of the North'. Dating to between 4000 BC and 3000 BC, the earthworks here are among the most awe-inspiring and oldest in Britain. The easiest to observe of these are the three 'henges', which form a mile-long chain aligned north-west to south-east.

THE THORNBOROUGH HENGES (CENTRAL).

Henge earthworks were created by building circular embankments around an inner ditch. The bank and ditch are interrupted by either one, two or several entrances, bridged by causeways. The examples at Thornborough are 200m-wide Class II henges. Such enclosures have two entrances opposite one another, giving them the appearance of a theatre in the round. These are the predominant henges of northern England, but they are most prevalent in North Yorkshire, where the densest collection in Britain survives. Additionally, the Thornborough Henges belong to, and lend their name to, a specific style of Class II henge, called the Thornborough Type (or Class IIA). These unusual henges have an additional thin ditch around the outside of their bank.

Of the three, the northernmost henge is the best preserved, but dense woodland hides it from view. This is no coincidence. According to nineteenth-century historian Thomas Langdale, the henge was intentionally preserved as far back as 1822. He wrote: 'The perfect one (the northern henge) ... was some years ago planted upon by the Earl of Ailesbury, by way of preserving it.' Despite the interest antiquarians showed to the henges, their descriptions, and resultant theories, were often fanciful. Thomas Pennant, who was among the first to describe the site in the early eighteenth century, believed they were built by the Vikings to be used as 'arenas for fighting duels'.

The central and southern henges are the most accessible of the three but are damaged. In particular, the southern henge has become gnarled over time, making it hard to discern from ground level. The central henge is better, but seems to have become a massive rabbit warren, with pockmarks burrowed all over its outer embankment. The best way – in fact, the only way – to appreciate the scale of the Thornborough Henges is to get up in the sky and observe them from an aerial perspective. Sunrise or sunset is also ideal, as shadows give contrast to the otherwise flat landscape, revealing the banks and ditches.

There are several theories on the purpose of Class II henges. Some early archaeologists believed they acted as defensive structures, quite like later hill forts. However, research has demonstrated that henges have little defensive function. Thanks to excavations across Britain, their relationship to religious sites, such as stone and timber circles, is now indisputable. Indeed, the greatest benefit of the Class II henge is not to block people from outside, but to block the landscape from within. Inside the henges at Thornborough, the modern landscape all but disappears. Only the sky and the causeways draw your attention, both of which point towards a common target: **the solstice sun**.

THORNBOROUGH'S SOUTHERN HENGE.

All three henges at Thornborough are aligned in a steep south-east–north-west configuration, with the entrances to their embankments facing one another. Their alignments are precise enough to suggest all three were used in conjunction. If this was the case, then we can assume some form of procession existed between them. Like in the aisle of a church, people may have walked between the causeways during key dates. As they align towards the south-east, they were likely built to mark the winter solstice.

Henges and Cumbrian circles (see Commondale Stone Circle) were built across Britain between 3200 BC and 2500 BC, during the mid to late Neolithic, a time of great religious revolution. In the same way that churches, synagogues and mosques allow congregations, so too did these prehistoric enclosures.

Communities could gather here, isolated from the landscape. With the open skies above, they may have worshipped those who granted them their food, shelter and worldly existence. Like Christmas, Al-Hijra or Passover, key dates for their respective religions, for Neolithic Britons the solstices may have been days to gather at henges to celebrate a religious holiday.

To better understand Neolithic activity at Thornborough, we must first understand the landscape. While the henges survive on the surface, other features remain in the form of crop marks, where dried out soils reveal where trenches were dug in the past.

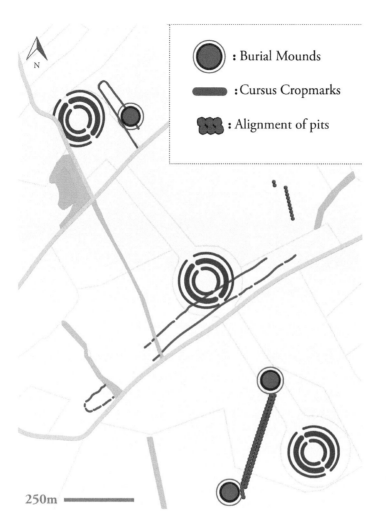

A PLAN OF THE
THORNBOROUGH
LANDSCAPE.

First, to the immediate south of the village is a Neolithic mortuary enclosure. This was an earthwork used to expose the dead to the elements, stripping bodies down to their bones, then to be deposited into burial monuments. Curiously, no Neolithic burial monuments have been found at Thornborough. It is unknown where the human remains from Thornborough's mortuary enclosure were taken after excarnation. To the north of the enclosure there are several lost barrows but nineteenth-century excavations proved these to be Bronze Age. Neolithic burial monuments do exist in the Vale of Mowbray. Ten kilometres south-east, at Low Barn, there are the crop mark remains of a lost Neolithic long barrow, alongside four lost henges. These are known as **Cana Barn, Tenlands, Low Barn** and **Dishforth**.

Second, there are two Early Neolithic earthworks known as cursus monuments at the site, one south of the northern henge and a second west of the central henge. Cursus monuments are covered in greater detail in Chapter 4 (see Rudston) but put simply these were long earthen enclosures created near the beginning of the Neolithic (est. 3800 BC). There has been little study of the examples found at Thornborough, but excavations in the 1940s and '50s revealed that Early Bronze Age burials had been placed within them.

Third, and most visible on hot days, is a curious alignment of pits snaking north to south around the central and southern henges. Within these pits, packing stones were found, which were likely used to hold either wooden posts or standing stones in place. These pits were investigated in 1994 by the Vale of Mowbray Project, led by archaeologist Jan Harding, along with the other crop marks mentioned. The monuments at Thornborough were treated not as individual sites but as parts of a single complex. It is believed the monuments were interconnected, added one after the other throughout prehistory, as beliefs evolved and the landscape demanded remodelling. Indeed, excavations at the pits revealed them to be of Early Bronze Age origin. This, along with the Early Bronze Age burials found within the cursus monuments, may suggest a continuity of use at Thornborough, between the Early Neolithic and the Early Bronze Age (3800 BC to 2000 BC).

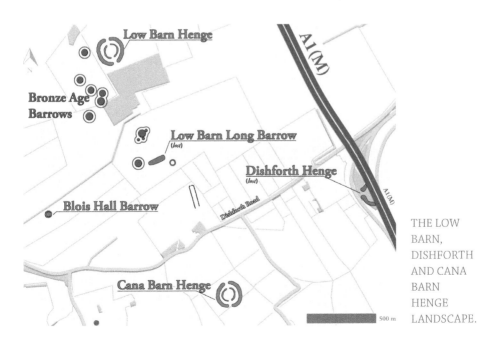

THE LOW BARN, DISHFORTH AND CANA BARN HENGE LANDSCAPE.

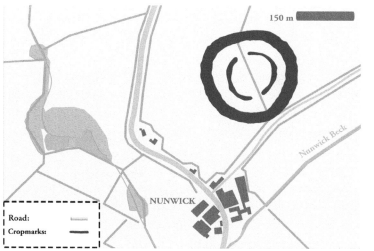

NUNWICK
HENGE.

Finally, Thornborough's position, at the centre of the Vale of Mowbray, marks an important crossroads. Here, beside the River Swale, is the easiest point between Cumbria, East Riding and the Peak District. Artefacts discovered in Neolithic pits at the site attest to trade between northern England's east and west coasts. Polished stone axes, originating in the Langdale Valley of the Lake District, have been unearthed here, alongside flint tools sourced from the Yorkshire coast. A landscape where communities from opposite sides of England met and traded. Whether or not these diverse communities worked on the henges together remains up for debate. However, studies observing modern megalith-erecting tribes have shown trade and cooperation between communities to have been a primary reason for monumental building projects.

THE DEVIL'S ARROWS

SE 39101 66534

Among the most impressive standing stones in Europe, the Devil's Arrows are a sight to behold. Taller than those at Stonehenge by only a slight margin, they hold the distinction of being the second tallest in Britain. They lie next to the town of Boroughbridge, east of the A1(M). Like most stone rows, it is agreed that the Devil's Arrows date to either the Late Neolithic or Early Bronze Age (est. 3200– 800 BC).

The three megaliths tower over Boroughbridge in a north-west to south-east aligned row. The central and northernmost stones stand in an open field, while the south stone stands in the woodland next to the road into town. Of the three, the central stone is the largest, standing at a mammoth 6.8m (22ft 6in). The southmost stone is similar, at 6.7m (22ft), and the northernmost stone is smaller at 5.4m (18ft). Each stone exhibits a weathered top with sharp grooves gnarled into the otherwise smooth sandstone. We can assume they once stood taller because of this.

They are not equidistant from each other. The south stone is almost twice as far from the central stone as the north stone, suggesting that several stones are missing. Antiquarian John Leland noted the stones in the sixteenth century. He described five megaliths, which formed a longer row leading northward. He also noted how a stone once occupied the area near the centre stone, in the gap between that and the south. Thirty years later, famed antiquarian John Camden surveyed the site, witnessing only the three we see today. He stated: 'One was lately pulled down by some that hoped, though in vain, to find treasure.'

THE CENTRAL STONE.

THE NORTHERN
STONE.

According to Camden, the stone was then broken up and used to repair a bridge across the nearby River Ure. This is, of course, a great shame, as these stones had travelled a great distance to be erected here. Researchers believe the Arrows were quarried 14km south at the Plumpton Rocks, a sandstone outcrop. It is estimated to have taken around 200 labourers six months to transport the stones over such a distance. Why this stone was chosen is not known, but the lack of suitable boulders in the Vale of Mowbray may be the key. Eastern England, unlike its western coasts, does not contain many large, loose boulders. Instead, sedimentary, earth-fast rocks like sandstone and limestone are far more common. If those who erected these megaliths needed stones this large, they would have had to source them from far away.

As for their purpose, several hypotheses exist. A classic theory on the purpose of stone rows is that they were used like crosshairs, drawing the observer's gaze towards the solstice sun. Serving a purpose like a calendar, these solstice alignments would signal the beginning of summer or winter. For a society reliant on farming, this would be crucial. Because the Devil's Arrows point south-east, many believe these stones signalled the beginning of winter.

Yet, despite solstice alignments occurring here, the Devil's Arrows are not easily used as crosshairs. The tall and varying heights of the stones mean their peaks do not align with the horizon from ground level. Indeed, it would be difficult to track a sunset or sunrise from here without a ladder. At any rate, why would people build something so simple and utilitarian, so large?

Unfortunately, the site's incompleteness halts any effort to decode its purpose. While there were five stones here in the sixteenth century, no one knows how many were lost between then and the Neolithic (a space of 5,000 years). No doubt the expansion of nearby towns caused the loss of earthworks in the area. Any attempt to understand these stones, which may be a single component of a lost complex of monuments, is hampered by a lack of context.

THE DEVIL'S ARROWS.

Even so, if we are willing to take a more open-minded approach, there are several larger alignments to be seen here. Looking from an aerial perspective, the Arrows are not as secluded as they seem. Following the south-westerly alignment, through the entrances of the Thornborough Henges (10 miles north), will direct you with near-pinpoint accuracy towards the Arrow's central stone. This 11-mile line also crosses through both entrances of the lost **Nunwick Henge**, which sits in alignment between Thornborough and the Arrows. It was excavated in 1961 by D.P. Dymond, who found that it was not a Thornborough-type henge as it lacked an external ditch.

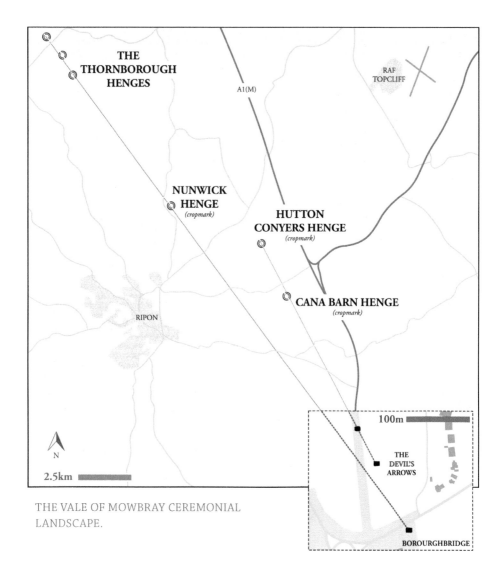

THE VALE OF MOWBRAY CEREMONIAL LANDSCAPE.

The alignments do not stop there. North of the Devil's Arrows, west of the A1(M) and Langthorpe, you can find the crop mark remains of a massive earthwork enclosure. This enclosure, seldom discussed, may be the vestiges of a superhenge, a Neolithic enclosure. There are few known examples of such earthworks in Britain. Famous examples include Durrington Walls and Avebury, both in Wiltshire, and Long Meg and Her Daughters in Cumbria. Aside from the Durrington Walls, little research has been done on these massive earthworks. Throughout the early to mid-Neolithic (est. 4000–3200 BC), they appear to have been associated with both settlement and ritual activity.

If you follow a north-westward alignment 8km (5 miles) from here, just east of Ripon, you will be directed to another set of crop marks. This time, you will be guided through a vast number of lost earthworks: **Cana Barn Henge**, **Copt Hewick Cursus** and **Hutton Moor Henge**. Travel another 8km (5 miles) in the same direction, and you will find a further enclosure at Ainderby Quernhow, known as **Sinderby Henge**. Then, 1.6km (1 mile) east of here, over the A1(M), there is the large **Stapley Hill Round Barrow**.

Following this alignment in the opposite direction, south-east from the Devil's Arrows, we hit another important spot in the landscape – the meeting point between the Rivers Swale and Ure – forming the River Ouse.

These alignments are not arbitrary, drawn between random points on a map (a spiritual premise known as ley lines). Instead, the Devil's Arrows and Thornborough Henges are a series of aligned monuments. With genuine, purposeful orientations, these sites point towards major features in the landscape. Their south-east to north-west alignment likely represents the marking of the solstice. This is on a scale unseen elsewhere in northern England.

PUDDING PIE HILL

SE 43697 81028

Pudding Pie Hill, one of England's grandest prehistoric mounds, is a rich and intriguing landmark, steeped in equal parts history and mystery. It lies east of Sowerby, just off the A168. To its west is Cod Beck, a small river that meanders into the River Swale to the south, joining the Ure east of the Devil's Arrows and forming the Ouse. Despite being encroached upon by the modern world, Pudding Pie Hill stands tall, a bold and unmistakable presence.

This is, or was, a burial mound, around 40m in diameter and 6m (20ft) tall. It is positioned within a floodplain at the tail end of a natural spur of land. Around its outer circumference is a ditch, which during heavy rainfall can become flooded like a moat. Such a mound fits the classic definition of a 'bowl barrow', a style of monument used throughout prehistory. However, as this is an enormous mound, we can assume it dates to either the Neolithic or Early Bronze Age (est. 3400–2500 BC), when shared burial spaces were common. Similar barrows are common in the nearby Yorkshire Wolds (see Chapter 4).

In 1855, the owner of the land, Lady Frankland Russell, excavated the top of the mound. Within her shallow trench were found the remains of three male skeletons, a heap of cremated remains and many Roman coins. Among these Roman finds were several rare artefacts dating to the early Anglo-Saxon period (est. AD 410–560): a shield boss, a shield handle and a spearhead.

Despite appearances, the mound is not the same age as the Roman and Saxon artefacts discovered within it. Instead, the artefacts were added thousands of years after the mound was created. Roman paganism encouraged offerings to supposed ancestors, making Roman activity at prehistoric burial mounds both expected and frequent across Europe. The Anglo-Saxon finds are a little more complex. Saxon activity at prehistoric sites is not unheard of, and they tended to favour burial mounds like this. Southside Mount, near Rudston (see Chapter 4), is a good example of the reuse of Bronze Age bowl barrows in Anglo-Saxon times. Like the Bronze Age Britons, Germanic pagans practised burials within earthen barrows. The most famous example is Sutton Hoo in Suffolk.

THE RIPON CAIRNS

Beyond Pudding Pie Hill, only a few burial mounds survive in the Vale of Mowbray. For the most part, evidence of Neolithic and Early Bronze Age burial practice is reserved to crop marks, many of which surround the henges in the area. However, three prominent burial cairns do survive within the centre of the vale. None of these are excavated and all are protected by law.

The largest of these – at 7ft tall (0.3m) – sits east of Kirklington, in woodland next to Stapley Lane. The other two are found on either side of the Cana Barn Henge complex. These are **Blois Hall Cairn** (SE 34812 72413) and **Hutton Conyers Cairn** (SE 35301 74335). Beyond their excellent state of preservation, there is little to note of these cairns. They exist on the uplands like other burial mounds, and in rows with other mounds they are aligned towards the solstice sunrise and fall.

OTHER SITES IN THE VALES OF MOWBRAY/YORK

CATTERICK COMPLEX

The landscape between Thornborough and Boroughbridge was not the only major prehistoric ritual complex in the Vale of Mowbray. Twenty kilometres (12 miles) north is the village of Catterick, home to a lost mega-complex of sites built around the River Swale. This included several large bowl barrows, henge earthworks, a cursus monument and a rare 'palisaded enclosure'.

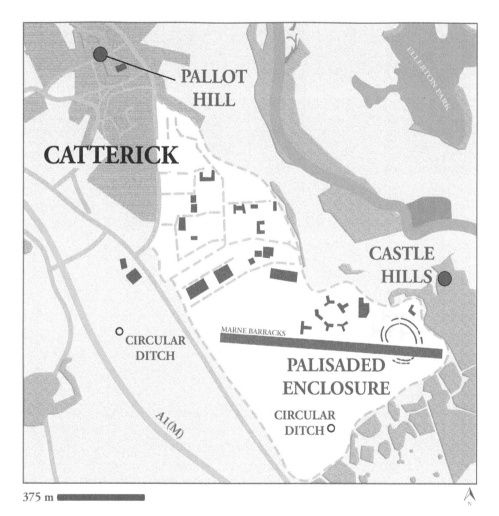

THE CATTERICK CEREMONIAL LANDSCAPE.

PALLET
HILL.

Palisaded enclosures are large arenas encircled by palisades (or big wooden walls). They are rare, with no examples surviving in the UK. They date to the mid to late Neolithic period (est. 3200–2500 BC), with the best-known example located south of Avebury Henge in Wiltshire. In 2004, the building of new barracks at the nearby Marne Barracks swallowed the enclosure at Catterick whole. Fortunately, archaeologist Duncan Hale and colleagues had investigated the enclosure before its destruction. The researchers discovered that the specimen was somewhat unique because it had a palisade built using 'paired posts', erected two-ply at equal intervals. Additionally, radiocarbon dates placed this enclosure quite late, in the Early Bronze Age, around 2530–2300 BC.

The henge, once found south of Catterick racecourse, was also special. Unlike typical examples, it consisted only of a bank of river cobbles, which were likely sourced from the Swale. This style of henge is rarer than even the palisaded enclosure. Only one other example is known in England, Mayburgh Henge, near Penrith, Cumbria. These are sometimes referred to as 'Irish henges', but such monuments are typically made from earth, not stone. As such, only this lost monument, and Mayburgh Henge, attest to this rarest of stone monuments. Antiquarian H. MacLaughlan reported the existence of the henge in 1849 as surviving 'within living memory'. However, a Roman road cutting through the henge possibly used its stones in construction, suggesting that it may have been damaged for over two millennia.

For those wanting a tangible piece of archaeology, there is hope. Pallot Hill (SE 23960 98042), a mound in the centre of Catterick, opposite St Anne's Church, is thought to have been part of a medieval motte-and-bailey castle. However, no such castle was ever recorded in the Domesday Book, and it is one of two unrecorded motte mounds at Catterick; the other resides near the palisaded enclosure at Marne Barracks. Therefore, these mounds may instead be immense prehistoric barrows, associated with the nearby henge, palisaded enclosure and Thornborough complex.

NEWTON KYME HENGE (TADCASTER)

SE 45890 44988

Yet another sister site to the henges at Thornborough, the Newton Kyme Henge is the most southerly of the Thornborough Type (Class IIA) henges in England. This example has the most ditches of the collection, three arranged concentrically within each other. The henge survives as a crop mark within a Roman military complex, between several forts. It has been suggested that the Romans may have used the henge as a marching ground or arena for gladiatorial games.

HARTWITH MOOR STONE

SE 21235 62741

Found buried in the soil when ploughing, the Hartwith Moor Stone was re-erected in a clearing east of Summerbridge in the mid-1960s. It apparently fell once more in the 1990s and was re-erected by the good folks at Highfield Farm. Whether this was a prehistoric standing stone is open to conjecture, though information on its origins is scant. The weathering on its top suggests it did stand upright for a period, and some have argued it displays cup and ring marks (though these appear natural).

DACRE BANKS ROCK ART

SE 18601 61645

Right on the cusp of the Yorkshire Dales, west of Dacre Banks, you can find a small moorland chock-full of wonderful rock art. The motifs here are among the most brilliant in Yorkshire and can be accessed by a nearby footpath. Particularly interesting are the so-called **Tadpole Stone** motifs, which resemble a tadpole, and **Morphing Rock**, which features an unusually large cup surrounded by a ring mark.

GILLING LONG BARROW

SE 60172 74169

Wedged between the Vale of York and East Riding, on the edge of the Howardian Hills, you can find a turbulent field of lumps and bumps. Though a mess today, this is the remains of a long barrow. It was excavated in 1867 by William Greenwell, who found little beside a few secondary burials containing pottery and flint tools. While the primary burial (for whom the barrow was originally built) was never located, Greenwell did describe the barrow as having a stone kerb, which no longer survives.

Like much of East Yorkshire, the area surrounding the long barrow is littered with archaeology, both Roman and prehistoric. The fields surrounding the long barrow are home to many Bronze Age round barrows, and chance finds during ploughing have turned up Bronze Age jewellery and Neolithic tools.

CHAPTER THREE

THE DALES AND CRAVEN

The Yorkshire Dales National Park is a collage of craggy outcrops, winding river systems and dank caves. This now iconic region has lent itself to romantic art and literature, as well as the greatest werewolf movie of the 1980s. Indeed, it is a stark and occasionally strange setting, owing in large part to its limestone geology. Walking in the Dales can, at times, feel like you are in an uncanny alien landscape. Yet, like many of the UK's greatest landscapes, the Dales' remoteness has helped preserve features of great antiquity.

Human bones dating to the Early Neolithic (est. 4000–3200 BC) have been found buried within the region's caves. Some believe Neolithic people used caves as ritual spaces, or even dwellings. As the region is unique in northern England for both its quantity and scale of cave systems, few comparable discoveries have been made elsewhere. But it is known that Neolithic people on the European continent occasionally used caves as burial spaces.

When deciphering ancient monuments, it is crucial to remember the concept of 'survivor's bias'. Most monuments built in bustling river valleys, now occupied by cities, motorways and reservoirs, have fallen victim to the ravages of time. On the other hand, smaller monuments located in isolated upland regions like the Yorkshire Dales have managed to endure. It is essential to remember that people didn't choose to live in inhospitable places. The seclusion offered by the Dales shielded the monuments from later destruction, providing us with a misleading perspective of where such monuments typically stood.

REETH

There has been debate about the origins of the place name Reeth. Some trace it to a Germanic or Viking origin, meaning 'area by the river'. Others derive the name from Celtic Cumbrian, translating it as 'ford'. In either case, both translations make clear what defines the area: the River Swale.

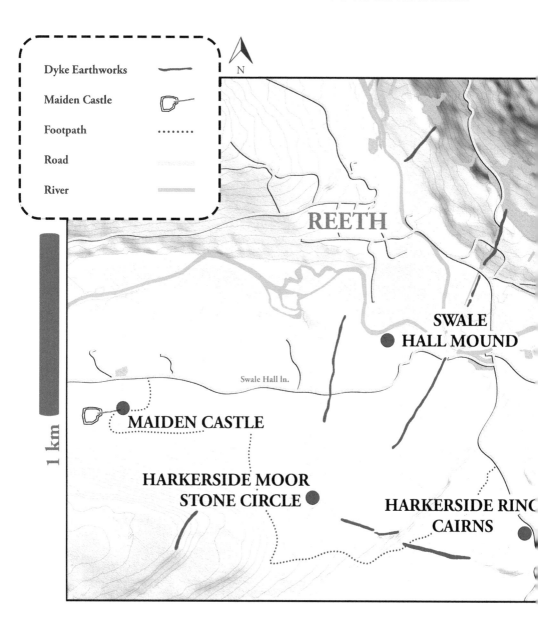

Dyke Earthworks

Maiden Castle

Footpath

Road

River

N

REETH

SWALE
HALL MOUND

Swale Hall ln.

MAIDEN CASTLE

HARKERSIDE MOOR
STONE CIRCLE

HARKERSIDE RING
CAIRNS

1 km

Swaledale, like much of Yorkshire, boasts a pastoral charm dating back to ancient times. Medieval archaeology dominates the visible landscape, with strip lynchets and ridge and furrow earthworks adorning the valley. However, aerial imagery reveals numerous Roman farmsteads scattered throughout the valley floor. Alongside the Roman presence are substantial defensive earthworks, ranging from the Iron Age to the Anglo-Saxon periods. The most extensive and intricate of these is the Grinton-Fremington Dyke System, spanning several kilometres across the valley. Despite limited knowledge about these earthworks, experts generally agree on an Anglo-Saxon origin as they intersect several Roman sites.

Beyond the Saxon and Roman remains, there are several prehistoric monuments higher up on the moors. These are both typical of the Neolithic and Bronze Age periods, and unusual in many ways. While much of the archaeology remains undated, there appears to have been a lot of activity occurring here during the Early Bronze Age (est. 2500–1800 BC).

MAIDEN CASTLE CAIRNS

SE 02185 98101

It should be impossible to discuss the history of the Dales without examining Maiden Castle. This colossal enclosure, which sits on the moor overlooking Grinton, is more interesting than its common name suggests. It is a neat embankment, formed with straight lines and curved edges, surrounded by a 4m-deep ditch.

For many, this feature is a hill fort, used by the Brigantes tribe during the Iron Age (est. 200 BC). But for others, such as archaeologist Jacquetta Hawkes, Maiden Castle represents 'not a fort' but a 'sacred enclosure'. Whatever the truth, Maiden Castle remains undated. Researchers cannot agree whether it belongs to the Iron Age, Roman or Anglo-Saxon period. For us, this means Maiden Castle does not belong in this book, as it was probably a later defensive enclosure, not a monument.

However, within the area, there are several authentic prehistoric monuments (pre-700 BC). A curious avenue, constructed using heaped stones, tapers off towards the east from the entrance of Maiden Castle. Next to

MAIDEN CASTLE AND ITS ADJACENT CAIRN

this distinctive feature lies a massive burial cairn, which we shall refer to as the Maiden Castle Cairn. It is one of the largest in England, with a diameter of 30m. Unfortunately, it has been mutilated, leaving its original size unknowable. Quarrying appears to be the obvious explanation for its terrible state of preservation. It seems the rubble avenue leading into Maiden Castle was built using stones from the cairn.

To the south-west of Maiden Castle lies another mound, a potential long cairn, concealed by dense moorland heather, and not marked on modern OS maps. The concept of long cairns will be explained in detail in the **Black Hill** section of this chapter, but, briefly, they were Early Neolithic burial cairns (est. 3600–3400 BC).

SWALE HALL BOWL BARROW

SE 03992 98523

The Swale Hall Bowl Barrow stands between two large stretches of the Grinton-Flemington dyke system on the edge of the River Swale. It can be accessed via Swale Hall Lane, which follows the river upstream east to west from Grinton. It sits on private land next to the hall, but you can easily view it from the foot-path to the immediate north (it is marked by an information plaque).

The barrow is situated on a lowland slope facing the river. It stands 30m in diameter along its widest axis and is 6m high. There are slight disturbances at its base due to medieval farming, but it is otherwise in good condition. While large bowl barrows tend to date to the Early Bronze Age, there exist even bigger examples, like this, in East Riding, dating to the mid to late Neolithic period (est. 3200 BC – see Chapter 4). Given the presence of the possibly Neolithic burial mounds up the hill at Maiden Castle, it may suggest the area was a Neolithic necropolis. The jury is still out, however.

Some questions remain. While bowl barrows are common across the UK, especially in lowland regions, the Swale Hall Bowl Barrow is a lonely monument, with no other comparable monuments in the lower valley. To find a similar mound, you must venture 2km up to Maiden Castle. Sitting as it does, between two large dykes, believed by many to be early medieval, one must wonder if the two are connected. One also must wonder if the mound is a burial feature at all, or if it is connected to the range of settlement earthworks scattered both north and south of the Swale. It is rare to find a burial monument surviving as prominent and untouched as this example, yet among such a palimpsest of archaeological features, it has had only its lower portion shaved away.

HARKERSIDE CIRCLE

SE 03534 97610

You can find this curious site buried in a sea of heather at the northern edge of Harkerside Moor. It sits on the brow of a plateaued spur of land, overlooking Swale Hall to the north. Approaching from the footpath to the south, it is easy to make out the most prominent stones of the circle, but it is easiest to approach from the west, venturing east along the spur. This also avoids the bracken, which will impede you if you attempt this in the summer months.

Harkerside Circle has been variously described as a ring cairn, a cremation cemetery, a stone circle and the base of a prehistoric hut (i.e. a 'hut circle'). While there are several hut circles in the area, most of which are linked to the nearby Maiden Castle, this is most likely not one of them. Although hut circles are roughly the same shape as this, there is a stone circle erupting from the perimeter of the banked enclosure, which itself may be a ring cairn.

Definitions of prehistoric monuments can get confusing, and the distinction between monument types can blur at times. In this case, what appears to be a ring cairn is topped by a stone circle. Such monuments are known as embanked stone circles, where a stone circle sits atop a ring cairn. Similar enclosures are common across northern England's uplands. Most surviving examples in England are found in neighbouring Cumbria, where sites such as Casterton Stone Circle and the Kirk share similar situations to Harkerside Circle, sitting on the brow of plateaued moors.

Author's note: The confusion between varieties of prehistoric circles may seem like a farce to many. Indeed, there is a trivial difference between, say, a ring cairn and a cremation cemetery. Nevertheless, during the Neolithic, and especially the Bronze Age, many monuments were circular. While the difference between a henge and a stone circle is obvious, the base of a round house can easily be confused for a ring cairn or stone circle.

With such sites, however, there should be a move towards a standardised vocabulary. One person's menhir is another's standing stone; one person's cromlech is another's stone circle; and one person's burial mound is another's tumulus or barrow. It is confusing, to say the least.

WENSLEYDALE

Wensleydale is the central valley of the Yorkshire Dales. It connects Cumbria to Yorkshire, linking the Irish Sea to the North Sea. This expansive valley boasts rolling limestone fells and offers a true taste of the Yorkshire Dales experience. Visitors can explore the imposing ruins of Bolton Castle near Redmire or delve into the depths of Semerwater.

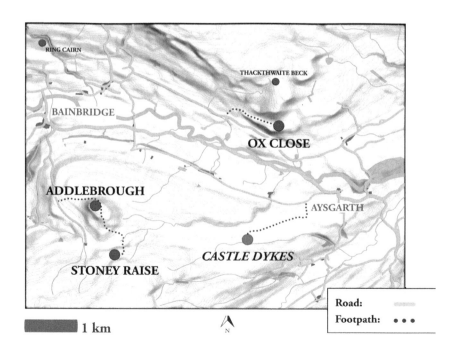

At the centre of Wensleydale is Aysgarth, a pretty village famous for its adjacent waterfalls, making it a popular spot for tourists. However, Aysgarth Falls are more than a pretty picture, as they are found near the middle of the River Ure. The Ure, of course, joins the River Swale at Boroughbridge, forming the River Ouse that flows through York. Perhaps because of this important riverine connection, the mountains surrounding Aysgarth Falls are home to some of North Yorkshire's grandest prehistoric monuments.

ADDLEBROUGH CAIRN

SD 94600 88124

Among other sites, Wensleydale boasts numerous stone circles, Bronze Age, Iron Age and medieval settlements, and several ring cairns. Despite this, there is a notable lack of prehistoric rock art in the area. However, there is one key exception to this. Atop Addlebrough Fell, a prominent flat-topped hill to the south of Bainbridge, you can find a very dense collection of decorated stones.

ONE OF ADDLEBROUGH'S DECORATED STONES.

Addlebrough Cairn, as we shall refer to it, sits in a sorry state of disfigurement. The stones were once the kerb of a cairn overlooking the Wensleydale Valley. The destruction of the cairn, which once sat between the stones, seems to have predated the nineteenth century, as antiquarians at the time described it as a druid circle, not a cairn as it originally stood. Judging by an 1861 account by travel writer Walter White, the site seems to have been further damaged around the time of the publication of his book, *A Month in Yorkshire*:

> *Here is, or rather was, a Druid circle of flat stones: but my companion screamed with vexation on discovering that three or four of the largest stones had been taken away, and were nowhere to be seen.*

As it stands today, the monument is a small arc of four stones, 6m in diameter. The arrangement of the stones is not thought to be original, as they appear to have been planted to make the rock art most presentable. This is further evidenced by a modern OS benchmark carved into one of the stones.

The art is typical of the Neolithic. In this case, we see three variations of the cup and ring motif: cups, rings and rosettes, a rarer combination of the two. Whether or not these cup-marked rocks were original to the cairn or reused due to their motifs, is not clear. It is likely this cairn is Early Bronze Age, and as such, these Early Neolithic motifs (est. 3500–3200 BC) would predate the cairn's construction by several centuries.

> **Author's note:** Just under Addlebrough's cliffs, to the west, is another stone I would be remiss not to mention: a natural boulder named the Devil's Stone. The reason this stone is named is not entirely understood as it is an undecorated, naturally situated boulder.

STONEY RAISE

SD 95062 86914

Stoney Raise is a colossal round cairn on Thornton Rust Moor, perched atop a low terrace overlooking Addlebrough. Reaching the cairn requires either a boggy walk over Addlebrough or via Carpley Green Road to the west. If you intend to visit **do not walk on the cairn**.

The cairn's size may be an indicator of its age. Small cairns containing the remains of one person can vary in age, between the early and middle Bronze Ages. Larger cairns, on the other hand, are more often older, either Neolithic or Early Bronze Age (est. 3000–2500 BC). Such cairns often contain many burials, interred within cists distributed within the cairn's mass.

Indeed, in the eighteenth century, travel writers described the existence of several cists along the cairn's outer edge. Within these cists, they detailed the discovery of loose bone fragments and several teeth, as well as a jewellery bead, from a necklace or bracelet. These artefacts went missing soon after their discovery and their exact specifications and dates have therefore been lost. Sadly, no traces of these cists survive either, despite photographs showing them as late as the 1990s. This is likely due to walkers trampling the cairn, knocking rocks into the divots where cists once existed.

Around its base is a kerb, indicating that its diameter (a whopping 34m) has remained the same since prehistory. However, the shape of the kerb, which has erupted outward on its eastern edge, may be due to antiquarian explorations within the cairn. These are not all accounted for, and we do not know the specific details of what they discovered or where they found it. Several divots in the top of the cairn, as well as the modern drystone wall running across its top, also suggest it has suffered damage in recent centuries.

Furthermore, there are compelling reasons to believe that Stoney Raise suffered damage or looting during prehistory. The cairn sits next to an impressive complex of settlement remains. These range from the Bronze and Iron Ages (1800–800 BC) through to the medieval period. It may be assumed that much of Stoney Raise's volume was quarried to build these settlements.

Author's note: Stoney Raise is the largest and most impressive round cairn I have encountered in northern England. Looking across the moor towards the cairn from the side of Addlebrough, the sheer scale of the cairn is breathtaking. There are few comparable monuments in England, and most outside, in Scotland, Wales and Ireland, are passage tombs. One comparable monument, known as Raiset Pike Long Cairn, lies 32km to the north-west, near the village of Orton in Cumbria. A Neolithic monument, Raiset Pike was found to contain the loose bones of several people, both adults and children.

OX CLOSE STONE CIRCLE

SD 99002 90132

Named after the old mining road it sits next to, Ox Close Stone Circle lies along the footpath north-east of Woodhall. Accessing the circle is simple and only requires a thirty-minute walk from Woodhall under Ivy Scar. The best view of the site is from the nearby hill to the north of the circle, which frames it in the foreground below the distant Height of Hazely. However, Ox Close Stone Circle is not a prominent monument, and good lighting is a must to appreciate its form.

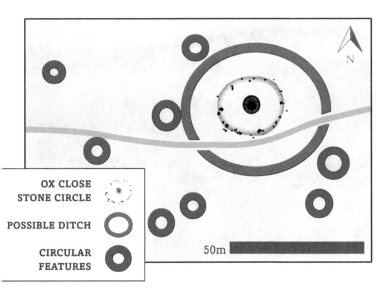

OX CLOSE STONE CIRCLE AND ITS ADJACENT ARCHAEOLOGICAL FEATURES.

OX CLOSE STONE CIRCLE

POSSIBLE DITCH

CIRCULAR FEATURES

50m

OX CLOSE STONE CIRCLE.

Archaeologists have described Ox Close inconsistently, as either an enclosed cremation cemetery or a banked enclosure. In either case, the identification of the site remains the same: a ring cairn of some variety. Ring cairns, as previously mentioned in this book, took many forms and were described in a variety of ways throughout history. In all cases, excavated ring cairns typically show evidence of burning, burial and repeated renovation during the Early Bronze Age.

If it is like other ring cairns, Ox Close would have enclosed funerary activity and rituals throughout the Early Bronze Age. We can assume cremations, excarnations and funerals took place here.

Yet, this is something of a unique specimen in Yorkshire. Firstly, the ring cairn, topped by unshapen limestone boulders, encircles a small burial cairn. Secondly, of the thirty-four stones that remain above ground, not one stands upright. The few archaeologists who have studied the circle have had conflicting opinions on whether the stones originally stood or not. The earliest investigation at the site, by Arthur Raistrick, concluded the stones had once been erected onto an embankment. This led him to believe the site was an embanked stone circle – a stone circle built upon a ring cairn.

There is a cairn at the centre of the circle, which may have held the charred remains of those who were cremated here. However, it is unclear whether this cairn was originally on the site or if it was added later. Neolithic and Early

Bronze Age stone circles often received secondary burials, added hundreds, or even thousands, of years after an enclosure's original use. An effortless way to increase the grandeur of a burial monument is to have it constructed in the centre of an already impressive site. Such customs are not unique to prehistory. Even today, burial at a prestigious site suggests a person was powerful or important (e.g. burials within cathedrals or within the grounds of an estate).

Author's note: Looking at the site via aerial imagery, there are several distinctive circular features around the circle that have survived as parch marks. This includes several possible hut circles or barrows, as well as a ditch around the stone circle's outer edge – perhaps a small Class I henge. However, when I first arrived at the circle in mid-November, I was met by an unusual sight. A concentric ring of white mushrooms had grown around the enclosure, a natural, though rare, phenomenon known as a fairy ring. Therefore, these features may be caused by mushroom blooms.

THACKTHWAITE BECK STONE CIRCLE

SD 98912 91211

This isolated stone circle stands at the centre of Carperby Moor. A winding track north of Carperby leads towards the site, which sits 2.5km from the village. Finding it is a challenge, especially during the summer months. The stones do not stand out in the landscape, as even the tallest stone is only ½m tall.

The circle is small, only 16m across. Six stones make up its circumference, evenly spaced, with the majority grouped to the east. The gaps in the circle's western quadrant are likely due to the removal of stones. But based on these gaps, we can infer that it once included around twelve stones. The function of circles like this is, surprisingly, well understood. In comparison to Cumbrian circles – the classic idea of a stone circle used as a ceremonial enclosure – smaller circles are often the remains of damaged burial monuments. Indeed, Thackthwaite Beck likely surrounds a buried cairn. This variety of monument, sometimes known as a burial circle, is the most common variety of stone circle in northern England.

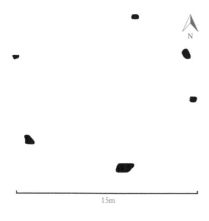

THACKTHWAITE BECK STONE CIRCLE AS SEEN FROM A BIRD'S-EYE PERSPECTIVE.

15m

Sadly, due to years of isolation on this well-farmed hillside, unstable structures such as cairns may have been lost. If you want to see an example of a complete monument of this variety, many examples do survive. In Cumbria, for instance, there are the White Moss Stone Circles, as well as the Lacra Circles. Additionally, next to the A6276, which crosses over the Pennines, you can find Lune Head Stone Circle. All examples, which date to the Early Bronze Age, include between twelve and sixteen well-spaced stones, which enclose an inner burial cairn.

CASTLE DYKES

SD 98228 87289

A curious circular trench lies at the apex of Flout Moor, to the west of Aysgarth. Access to the site is easy, as it can be visited via a well-kept trackway from Aysgarth. Known as Castle Dykes Henge, this feature might be a rare and fascinating example of a Neolithic Class I henge earthwork. Recent excavations at the site, however, have cast doubts on its origins, and it seems that appearances can be deceiving ...

CASTLE DYKES AS SEEN FROM ITS WESTERN EMBANKMENT.

For most of the past century, Castle Dykes was believed to be a Class I henge: a henge enclosure with a single entrance. From ground level, you can see this profile. A large ditch surrounds an island of earth, within a low circular embankment. On the east side of the embankment is the single entrance. Henge entrances typically open out onto a causeway, splitting the ditch in two. However, no causeway exists at Castle Dykes, and its east-facing entrance is unaligned with the solstice sun.

Castle Dykes is also bent out of shape. Its position and size make it dip over the sides of the small hill it perches on, like a dishcloth draped over a rolling pin. This makes its northern and southern sides droop below the hill's peak. Archaeologists often speculate that henge embankments served to block out the landscape, drawing one's gaze upwards, towards the sky. Castle Dykes' drooping embankments allow a full view of the surrounding landscape, revealing it in full panorama.

The earliest survey to classify the site as a henge was in 1948. Archaeologist R. Atkinson believed that, although no stones currently stood at the site, a stone circle may have existed within the earthwork. He posited: 'There is no sign of any stone structure in the central area, but the district abounds in stone walls, for which the site may have been robbed in the past.' This theory, that Castle Dykes was a henge, would remain gospel for seventy-one years.

However, earlier reports did not agree. Antiquarian Harry Speight was among the first to write about the site. He noted in an 1897 report how, 'from its low and simple form, as well as from its situation in Celtic territory, there seems little doubt that it was the work of these early people'. 'Celtic', in this early context, referred to all prehistoric Britons, but it seems Speight was referring to the regions inhabited by the Iron Age Brigantes tribe. A later article by Edmund Bogg in 1906 noted more blatantly how 'earthworks known as Castle Dykes ... probably Angle or Danish, although Roman relics have been found here'. Either an unpublished excavation or a chance find, had revealed Roman activity at the site.

In 2019, archaeologists published a detailed survey report of the site. This survey, led by Alex Gibson, would shift opinions on Castle Dyke's origin, all but confirming earlier doubts. Two core samples were taken, one from the inner ditch and another from the outer bank. When radiocarbon dated, these samples were shown not to be from the Neolithic, nor the Bronze Age.

Instead, Castle Dykes was revealed to date to approximately 400 BC: the **Iron Age**. Among the earth and stone in the ditch core, a minute jewellery bead was discovered. When the bead was analysed, it was found to be Roman. As the Iron Age led straight into the Roman period, Castle Dykes was likely occupied by people who owned Roman goods. This would suggest Castle Dykes was created over 2,500 years later than expected. A stark reminder of how fast ideas can shift after academic study.

YOCKENTHWAITE 'STONE CIRCLE'

SD 89977 79363

You can find this intriguing little monument between the hamlets of Yockenthwaite and Deepdale. To access the circle, you will need to either walk via Yockenthwaite Farm or scramble over the adjacent river. It sits next to the Dales Way path, where you can often find intrepid hikers taking a rest stop or eating their lunch within the circle.

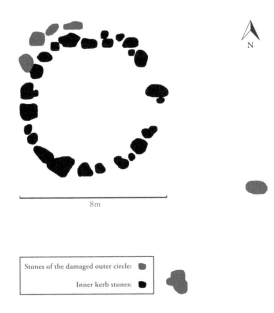

YOCKENTHWAITE STONE CIRCLE AND ITS POSSIBLE SECOND CIRCLE.

8m

Stones of the damaged outer circle:

Inner kerb stones:

While this is a circle made of stones, it is not a stone circle in the classical sense. Twenty-four limestone boulders make up its circumference, each boulder nearly touching the next. They sit on a raised mound, which may be a cairn or a natural heap from the adjacent hillside. Within this tight circle is a concave depression, where it seems some digging into the mound took place. Two stones to the south are often described as outliers, stones placed outside the circumference of the circle.

There are several theories on what the site's original purpose was, and in what period it was built. Curiously, many people refer to the monument as Yockenthwaite Ring Cairn; however, there are several issues with identifying this as a ring cairn. Firstly, the area within the circle is neither flat nor traversable. Congregations could not take place inside Yockenthwaite, making it a poor ceremonial enclosure. Secondly, the circle's form does not match that of a ring cairn. While the stones do sit atop a doughnut-shaped embankment, this appears to be a result of the digging. It seems the stones served as a kerb around this mound, holding it neatly in place.

Rather than a ring cairn or stone circle, what we see at Yockenthwaite may be a kerb cairn. These cairns are named after the tightly spaced stones that form their shape. Typically, kerb cairns are only small, but examples in neighbouring Cumbria have been known to exceed 15m in diameter. The divot at the centre of the circle, within the mound, may also suggest this feature was robbed sometime in the past.

Large kerb cairns, like this example, are often found at the centre of concentric stone circles, a rare style of burial monument, where two or more rings of stone are arranged within one another. The inner circle of these monuments is typically a kerb cairn. All examples have a burial mound as their central focal point. This suggests their outer circles either enclosed rituals targeting their inner kerb cairns or served to demarcate a boundary.

The two outlying stones to the south of Yockenthwaite may be key here, as their position is concentric with the circle. Furthermore, four stones placed against the circle's north-west quadrant appear to be out of place, as if moved inwards away from the field entrance. If extended outward, this would create a concentric circle of at least six stones, around 23m in diameter. This would also date the site to the late Neolithic/Early Bronze Age, as many concentric circles in Britain date to that period.

WHARFEDALE

Wharfedale is a land of striking contrasts and rugged beauty. In its winding valleys and craggy peaks, you can sense the deep history and enduring spirit of people long gone. It is a classic 'palimpsest landscape', edited repeatedly by the forces of both man and nature. Indeed, with its countless layers of visible archaeology, the valley has a sense of timelessness.

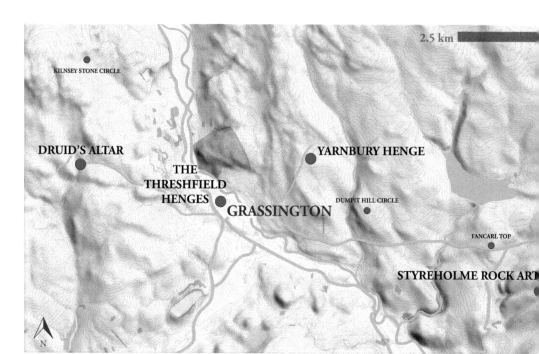

DRUID'S ALTAR.

The eponymous River Wharfe winds its way down the centre of this palimpsest, carving out a path that leads into the heart of the valley. Being situated at the gateway into the Dales from the south, Wharfedale likely saw a lot of traffic throughout prehistory. During the Roman occupation of Britain, a Roman road was built here, connecting Wharfedale to Wensleydale. This road, which linked Stake Moss to Bainbridge, may have been based on a pre-existing route, as it cuts close to the Bronze Age monuments on Addlebrough Fell.

At the centre of this large valley is Grassington, a quaint village famed for its cobbled streets and colourful gardens. On the slopes surrounding the village are some of the most striking archaeological landscapes in Britain. Earthworks overlaying earthworks, forming a palimpsest of prehistoric activity. Much of this is the result of Iron Age, Roman and medieval agriculture. But heading higher up the slopes, linear features give way to circles – the remnants of Bronze Age ritual activity.

DRUIDS' ALTAR

SD 94946 65275

Three megaliths stand high on Hammond Close, north-east of Bordley, the most prominent stones of a cairn known as Druids' Altar or Bordley Circle. They lay south of the road between Threshfield and Malham Cove.

The site is often described as a four-poster circle (see Chapter 1, Ramsdale Stones), a description that ignores the site's history. Accounts have varied over the centuries, but it seems a lot has changed since the earliest descriptions of the site. An 1848 map of Malham Moor, surveyed by R.E. Penrice, shows the Druids' Altar as a massive mound topped by at least six stones. Later, in 1892, antiquarian Harry Speight described it as a 'round stone and earth mound about 150ft in circumference and 3ft high ... formerly surrounded by a circle of upright stones, only three of which are now left standing'. Indeed, a 2007 investigation of the monument found evidence of a circle of stones around the monument. This may have served as the kerb of the 20m-wide burial mound.

Speight also stated how 'on one side, there was a large flat stone resting upon two others'. Similar arrangements of stone, where flat stones form lintels supported by others, are known as dolmens. They are the surviving

chambers of Neolithic burial mounds. Yet, in this case, the stones were located on the exterior, a potential portal into the mound. Unfortunately, by the twentieth century, this stone had vanished, leaving only a rough circular frame in its wake. However, a large flat stone lies just 6m south of the monument, which may correspond to the lintel mentioned by Speight.

If this was an entrance, it may have aligned the site towards the solstice sun in mid-Neolithic fashion (est. 3200 BC). From Hammond Close, on the winter solstice, you can witness the sun set behind Weets Top, a prominent hill to the south-west. Similar alignments exist at many Neolithic burial mounds. The best-known examples of solstice alignments are those found in Neolithic tombs, such as Maeshowe on Orkney. There, you can observe the winter solstice sun setting behind the hills of Hoy.

Author's note: The field in which the Druids' Altar sits contains a vast complex of settlements, standing stones and field systems. Two settlements, known as Hammond Close to the south and Lantern Holes to the north, are best appreciated via satellite imagery.

YARNBURY HENGE

SE 01406 65417

Yarnbury Henge lies north-east of Grassington. You can follow Moor Lane up towards Grassington Moor, either driving or walking up from Grassington via several footpaths. Make sure to approach the henge in good lighting, as the level of awe generated is a league of magnitudes greater at either sunrise or sunset.

YARNBURY HENGE.

Yarnbury is a Class I henge, a henge with only a single entrance. Like Class II henges, Class I henges likely enclosed religious gatherings. The activities involved in such gatherings could be discussed in infinite detail with infinite conjecture. For the sake of simplicity, I will simply state that **we do not know**. What we do know, however, is that henges often align towards features in either the landscape or the sky. In this case, the single entrance opens out towards the south-east. This aligns the henge to the winter solstice sunrise. Many Neolithic and Early Bronze Age sites in northern England share this alignment.

While not documented, it seems an early excavation took place at Yarnbury in 1922. This is evidenced by a square depression at the centre of the henge. Allegedly, Bronze Age urn fragments were unearthed during this dig, which are periodically on display as the Yarnbury Urns at Manchester Museum. In

A MEGALITH LYING AT THE HENGE'S ENTRANCE.

1964, a better recorded excavation was overseen by archaeologist D. Dymond. During the dig, the researchers uncovered that the ditch had been dug deep into the bedrock. They also found that the outer bank resulted from dumping the earth and stone directly outside the trench.

A remarkable excavation took place between the spring and summer of 2014 by students at the University of Bradford. Led by Alex Gibson, the excavation team investigated a square anomaly to the south-east of the henge that, upon analysis, was found to be an Early Neolithic dwelling.

Dating to approximately 3600 BC, the dwelling investigated at Yarnbury is among the oldest yet found in the UK. While this does not date the henge, which likely dates to around 3000 BC, it does give some context to the landscape in which it sits. Just by glancing at a satellite view of Grassington Moor, north of Grassington, it is easy to see how bustling with activity the hillside was throughout prehistory. While now we may only see walled enclosures, thrown up in the eighteenth and nineteenth centuries, with an aerial perspective earthwork patterns can be seen with incredible clarity across the moor. Such palimpsest landscapes are found subtly throughout Britain. But here, on these relatively undisturbed moors, evidence of layer upon layer of surviving archaeology can be seen poking up through the grass.

Author's note: The archaeological footprint on Grassington Moor ranges from the Neolithic to the medieval period, and beyond. It is important to remember that each of the cultures following the previous would have known of, and interacted with, the very same features in the landscape. The remains of this house would have been as ancient to the builders of Yarnbury Henge as medieval sites are to us. Therefore, the choice to build a grand religious enclosure so close to what they would perceive as antiquity should be viewed with intrigue.

Two more potential Class I henges sit 5km west of Yarnbury, either side of Skirehorns, and the two sites share Yarnbury's east-facing alignment. Knowledge of these, as well as the nearby Threshfield sites, was aided by aerial laser-scanning technology, known as LiDAR. With the use of this technology, archaeologists may detect slight differences in the height of the ground, exposing previously hidden earthworks beneath the vegetation.

STYREHOLME ROCK ART

Several panels of Neolithic rock art are found to the east of the village of Appletreewick, on the aptly named Pock Stones Moor. The stones, which are scattered between Nursery High and Burhill, are easy to find, as many stones in the landscape display deep and complex cup mark motifs.

The Styreholme Carvings, as they have come to be known, are located along the footpath leading between Stump Cross Caverns and Styreholme. Only one of the stones, found lodged in a wall, can be viewed from the path. But thankfully, all the stones sit on open-access land, and you are free to explore each of them as you please. This too is easy, as the rock art lies on the moor's most prominent boulders. It can be quite fun to walk between the moor's boulders, anticipating whether you will find a prehistoric motif or not. Often you can find at least a single cup.

A CARVED ROCK AT SE 07790 61840.

FANCARL TOP STONE CIRCLE

SE 06432 63052

Also known as the Appletreewick Stone Circle, due to its proximity to the village, this little circle lies just south of Grimwith Reservoir. Despite sitting just off the B6265, its position over the crest of Fancarl Top makes viewing it impossible from the road. Unfortunately, it is also located on private land. Therefore, I would suggest enjoying it from the comfort of this book. Thankfully, for those who feel deprived by not seeing this circle in person, it is lacklustre.

At least four ring cairns were built on the same hillside, which were likely used during Early Bronze Age funerals, particularly cremations. We may assume the stone circle served a similar purpose and, like Thackthwaite

Beck Stone Circle near Aysgarth, Fancarl Top may be the remains of a burial circle. However, curiously for an Early Bronze Age necropolis, there are no round barrows or cairns on the hill.

> **Author's note:** Before photographing this circle, I had believed it was positioned on Fancarl Top for its terrific views south-west. However, I was surprised to find sweeping views from the circle completely blocked to the south. Instead, it sits among a bleak landscape facing north. Early Bronze Age burial monuments often face the valleys of their builders, so there is the possibility there is more to find among the seemingly barren moors surrounding Grimwith Reservoir.

THE THRESHFIELD HENGE COMPLEX (LOST)

SD 98763 64253

Up until recently, Yarnbury and Castle Dykes were believed to be the only henges in the Yorkshire Dales. However, as archaeological science has progressed and methods of spatial analysis have evolved, this belief has been thoroughly squashed. Not only was Castle Dykes not a henge, but it now seems Yarnbury was far from a lonely monument. Additionally, just down the hillside from Yarnbury, in the unassuming village of Threshfield, archaeologists discovered a complex and impressive array of henges.

Unlike Castle Dykes, which was proven to be an Iron Age settlement, Yarnbury was proven to be a genuine henge via multiple excavations. This originally presented a conundrum, however, as henges are very rarely situated in upland areas, especially not on the crest of a steep hill. Thankfully, the discovery of the Threshfield Henges provided some context for the area's Neolithic activity. The site was discovered following Alex Gibson and colleagues' survey work, which was published in the *Archaeological Journal* in 2017.

The largest and best-surviving of the earthworks is a Class II henge, labelled by the surveying team as Threshfield Henge 2. While near impossible to see on the ground today, even in ideal lighting, the henge survives slightly, and can be recognised via aerial imagery. While its shape and scale are easily noted from an

aerial perspective, its alignments were only made clear using magnetometry, a method of ground scanning. Looking at the data, archaeologists could discern an earthwork like the henges at Thornborough: a Class IIA henge, with both an internal and external ditch. Like Thornborough, Threshfield Henge 2 aligns to the south-west, towards the winter solstice sunrise.

To the north-east of Henge 2, there was Henge 1. This appears to have been a similar earthwork, featuring two concentric ditches. However, not only does this earthwork seem to lack an entrance, but the space between ditches suggests it also lacked an embankment. To add to the peculiarities of this feature, an inner ring of pits was identified by the team. These were either a stone circle, a timber circle or an arrangement of burial pits. In any case, the pits do not run concentric to the earthwork, suggesting they are either older or younger than the ditches. Unbroken circular earthworks with inner pit alignments are not unheard of. The most famous of these features is Stonehenge, which has an outer ring ditch. But other examples survive near Penrith, Millom and Bootle in Cumbria, as well as the Ring of Brodgar on Orkney.

Finally, there is a large mound, or cairn, located to the south-east of Henge 2. Aligned parallel to the orientation of Henge 2's entrances, this cairn is the best preserved and most obvious remaining feature at Threshfield. It is one of two Neolithic cairns in the Grassington area, both of which sit in the area between Threshfield and Yarnbury Henge. It would seem that by the Early Bronze Age, an identifiable tract of land stretching from the River Wharfe up to Yarnbury to the north-east was dominated by Neolithic monuments.

KILNSEY MOOR

SD 95124 68034

High up on Kilnsey Moor, far from the nearest footpaths, lies an almost mythical collection of prehistoric remains. While seldom mentioned, even in academic literature, most of these seem to be settlement remains, Bronze Age field systems and roundhouses. The majority are concentrated around Dowkerbottom Cave, which howls over the northern edge of the moor. This includes at least three Early Bronze Age ring cairns, which are positioned to the west of the cave.

Perhaps the most noteworthy feature is a small stone circle, the stones of which remain at the centre of the moor. This is a ruinous burial monument of some variety, surviving as six stones surrounding a low mound.

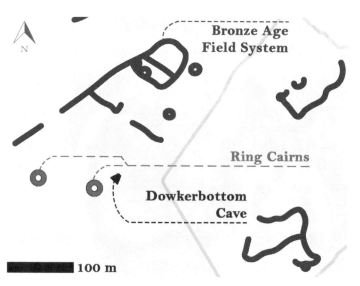

Bronze Age Field System

Ring Cairns

Dowkerbottom Cave

100 m

THE MONUMENTS AND FIELD SYSTEMS SURROUNDING DOWKERBOTTOM CAVE.

ILKLEY MOOR

Among England's best-loved uplands, Ilkley Moor, situated between Ilkley and Keighley, is certainly a tract well travelled. While the moor does not sit within the Dales, the town of Ilkley does, serving as the starting point of the Dales Way. Characterised by its millstone grit, a greyish sandstone, this landscape is frequented by visitors all year round. What many of these visitors may not know is that they are walking among some of Europe's most important prehistoric art ...

Between the rolling hills of Ilkley Moor a wealth of rock art motifs stands out, record-breaking in their abundance. You can find over 400 decorated rocks here, each boasting designs that vary from simple cup marks to intricate swirls. These motifs are typical of the Neolithic era, featuring cups, rings, tails and linear lines. However, a few unique designs do stand out. Interestingly, these more intricate motifs appear more frequently in areas that are easier to reach, along natural pathways. This has led some to believe that some of the rock art was created with more effort, because its creators intended for it to be seen by a larger audience. This theory implies that Ilkley Moor was widely traversed throughout prehistory.

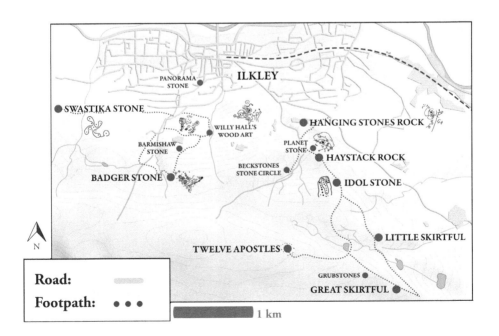

There are many burial cairns found here. The Green Crag Necropolis, located to the east of the moor, is distinct from the rock art; it is a space where people chose to honour their dead. Along this corner of the moor, activity dating back to the Neolithic has been found. Polished stone axes originating from the Lake District, dated between 3800 BC and 3200 BC, have been found close to several Bronze Age cairns. Evidently, this moor saw human activity for thousands of years.

Due to the sheer amount of rock art here, we cannot cover every single example in this section. For the most part, the designs are simple cup and ring motifs typical of the Neolithic. We will focus on a select few sites that give a good impression of the range of designs on the moor. Because Ilkley Moor is made up of moorland hills, the monuments, which are clustered near the moor's centre, can be difficult to find. Clear weather conditions and a fundamental level of preparation is advised if you wish to hike between the sites listed in this section.

HANGING STONES ROCK

SE 12822 46766

The rock art on Hanging Stones Rock, at the far north-east corner of Ilkley Moor, is one of the stranger rock art motifs in England. Two separate motifs are found here, each surrounded by modern graffiti.

The motifs are better rendered than most other examples on the moor and they are unusually large. The patterns are each centred around a cup and ring mark. From this central motif, several labyrinthine lines project and curl, creating an expanding arc of carvings. The largest example has a single line protruding from its side, linked like the trunk of a tree to several cup and ring marks.

Author's note: As abstract designs like these are open to endless speculation, it may be a fool's errand to interpret the meaning behind the motif. However, regarding the art itself, it is easier to speculate on its stylistic merits. The art only barely fits into the cup and ring tradition, and there are few parallels in passage tomb art. Therefore, Hanging Stones Rock is a special artistic expression – breaking a typically rigid formula. Today, we often find artistic rule breakers more compelling than their derivative counterparts. Prehistoric people may have felt the same.

THE TWELVE APOSTLES

SE 12610 45066

There are very few stone circles in Yorkshire; megalithic temple-like enclosures with a traversable space at their centre (sometimes called Cumbrian Circles). Enclosures where religious ceremonies were performed, whether for the living or the dead. The Twelve Apostles, which sits at the east of Ilkley Moor, is often counted among such circles.

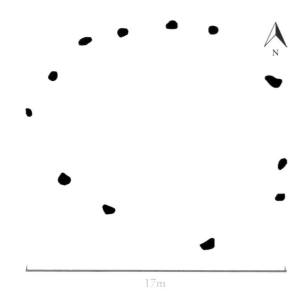

THE TWELVE APOSTLES AS SEEN FROM A BIRD'S-EYE PERSPECTIVE.

Twelve stones stand in a 17m-wide arrangement. While there is often speculation about this layout, the circle's current form is the result of modern restoration. Arthur Raistrick (explorer of Ox Close Stone Circle in Wensleydale) visited the site around the turn of the twentieth century, describing twenty stones that made up its circumference, along with one at its centre. There was no mention of a central stone in earlier descriptions, so this stone was most likely misplaced at that time.

Raistrick also noted an 'earthen bank' around the base of the stones. This may imply the Twelve Apostles was once an embanked stone circle – an Early Bronze Age variety of ring cairn. As neither this bank nor the stone count survives, we must assume the current appearance of the circle is nothing like the original. In fact, by the 1960s, every single stone in the circle had fallen or disappeared into the overgrowth. It was only after an unauthorised restoration in 1971 that it took its modern D-shaped form. Almost none of the stones are in their original positions, and several stones that were once on their sides now stand upright.

Author's note: Contrary to popular opinion (which sees the circle as a grand temple-like enclosure), the circle was likely a small funerary enclosure; possibly a variety of ring cairn known as an embanked stone circle. As the Twelve Apostles sit to the east of the moor, among the Green Crag Necropolis, it would seem they are connected to funerary activity. What was originally a ring cairn was embellished with a stone circle; later, a small round cairn was added to its centre, making it a burial circle.

GRUBSTONES STONE CIRCLE

SE 13648 44722

You would be forgiven for walking straight past this unassuming circle. Located between the Twelve Apostles and the Skirtful of Stones, it lies south of the prominent Grubstones Crag. Heading south, past the nearby outdoor activity hut, is a straightforward way to find it. A similar site sits 1.2km to the south, known as the Horncliff Circle, which is more clearly a ruinous kerb of a burial monument, having been built on an exposed slope.

It is well hidden among the heather, and a grouse butt has devoured the south-west third of it. Twenty stones survive in the monument's current state, forming a closely spaced ring 12m in diameter. On first inspection, this looks like a stone circle, with an entrance and an inner traversable space. This is an unfortunate result of disfigurement, however; the circle would have looked far different in prehistory.

J. Colls, esteemed antiquarian, excavated the site in 1846. He revealed a square feature at the centre of the circle. Although not understood at the time, this was probably a cist. No remains of this structure appear to survive today, but anti-quarian sketches show it was around 2m wide. Cremated remains were found within, alongside a 'flint spearhead'. The combination of an individual cremation within a cist – a Bronze Age custom – and Neolithic tools suggests an Early Bronze Age date, consistent with a kerbed tumulus.

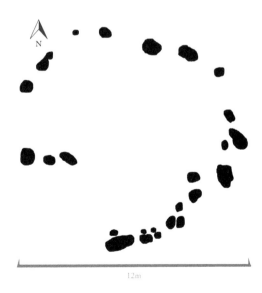

Otherwise, this may be an example of a burial circle, like the nearby Twelve Apostles. Burial circles often stand twelve-to-16m in diameter, formed of closely placed stones. They typically contain a small burial cairn, sprouting from the centre of the circle. This would have been a concentric design, mirrored in the nearby rock art: a circle within a

12m

THE GRUBSTONES FROM ABOVE.

circle. No inner cairn survives here today, but as evidenced by the disappearance of the Grubstones' cist, such features are easily lost over time.

Author's note: Not only is a third of the circle missing, but an 'orgone accumulator' was built into its side in the early twentieth century. But what is an orgone accumulator? According to proponents of some early twentieth-century alternative medicines, orgones are the forces of life and sexuality that you can harness and store within inanimate objects. The Grubstones were no doubt converted because of their association with the paranormal.

THE SWASTIKA STONE

SE 09560 46972

The Swastika Stone sits on a crag overlooking Ilkley, within the north-western edge of the moor. It is very weathered, and only visible in perfect lighting. Your best option is to view the Victorian replica, which sits on a separate stone in front of the motif.

The motif is comprised of two elements. First, there is the swastika. Unlike the well-known, and infamous, twentieth-century symbol, this motif is swirling and rounded, more of a lauburu than a swastika. It has four bulbous arms, swelling from a central junction. From one of these arms comes a tail, joining a cup and ring mark. Second, there are the cup marks. Unlike common cups, these do not vary in size throughout the motif. They are small and well formed. Each cup is positioned around the motif: one in each arm, one in the centre and one between each arm. Again, this is unlike typical cup mark arrangements, which are less symmetrical in their placement.

While Neolithic rock art is rarely emblematic outside of cups and rings, this symbol was clearly created by design. Unlike typical free-flowing cup and ring patterns, there appears to be a genuine artistic vision here. When compared to other carvings on Ilkley Moor, this swastika appears more driven and deliberate in its design.

THE SWASTIKA STONE'S REPLICA
(THE CRAG IN THE BACKGROUND HOLDS THE ORIGINAL).

LEFT: A SKETCH OF THE SWASTIKA STONE'S MOTIF.

BELOW: ON THE LEFT: SUTTON CHURCH GRAFFITI, ENGLAND; ON THE RIGHT: CAMUNIAN ROSE, ITALY.

So, what is it? Well, first we should tackle the theory that it is prehistoric. For a long time, it has been believed the Swastika Stone was created during the Bronze Age. This motif may be one of the last gasps of the cup and ring tradition. During the Bronze Age, other rock art hotspots in Britain, such as Ireland and Cumbria, began to decorate only metals, wood and pottery. Nonetheless, people in West Yorkshire may have continued pecking at rocks for over a millennium.

This continuation allowed a union of designs to manifest as traders from Europe entered England more frequently to do business. The Camunian Rose, a motif found among the Italian Valcamonica rock art, is a good example of this. The Camunian Rose exhibits the exact same design as the Swastika Stone, yet is often dated to the Iron Age/Roman period (est. 100 BC–AD 100), far too late for cup and ring marks. Given the turbulence of those periods, it is possible (if unlikely) that troops from the Valcamonica region ended up stationed near Ilkley Moor.

Conversely, there is good evidence to suggest this swastika motif is not prehistoric at all. Across Europe you can find these exact symbols in medieval settings. Most are associated with Germanic paganism (a contentious topic in this context, to say the least), with examples found in Viking contexts in Tossene, Sweden. Two of the best examples are found in Britain: a graffito at Little Waltham Church in Essex and another in Sutton Church, Bedfordshire, both dating between AD 900 and 1350.

These late examples may represent a form of medieval folk paganism, possibly a representation of superstitious characters. The graffito within Sutton Church displays the same swastika carved upon the chest of a human figure, whom some have interpreted as Odin. As is evident at many sites listed within this book (see Pudding Pie Hill), the Anglo-Saxons often took interest in prehistoric sites. While Anglo-Saxons are unlikely to have carved the Swastika Stone themselves, their cultural ancestors may have retained their folklore. Perhaps, after noticing a moorland with plentiful rock art, a medieval rambler (est. AD 900–1350) doodled this symbol around an already present cup mark. The jury is still out ...

Author's note: As Italy was likewise occupied by Germanic invaders, this may also explain the Camunian Roses. The Valcamonica rock art is believed to date between the Neolithic and medieval period. So, there is certainly a case for all swastika motifs being of a later date.

THE PLANET STONE

SE 12961 46398

Among a collection of boulders, at the base of the hill below Haystack Rock, you can find the Planet Stone. Also known by some as the Map Stone, due to its resemblance to a map, the stone's abstract motif is beautifully realised. Sadly, it is weathered and hard to see in broad daylight. Ten small cup marks, each surrounded by a ring, are joined by a network of lines. They surround a central depression in the rock, appearing like planets orbiting a star. The line continues up the north side of the boulder, following the edge of the stone. The south side is framed by a natural lip in the rock, which seems to have been used to frame the artwork.

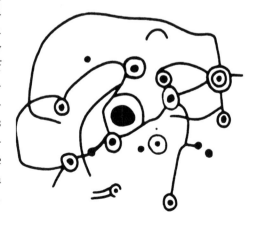

A SKETCH OF THE PLANET STONE MOTIF.

BACKSTONE BECK ROCK ART / 'STONE CIRCLE'

SE 12597 46139/SE 12738 46251

Two features of note survive south of Green Crag, west of Backstone Beck. One is a panel of rock art, the other is a dubious collection of upright stones. Finding them is easy as a footpath heading southward from the Dales Way cuts directly past them.

THE SUPPOSED STONE CIRCLE AT BACKSTONES BECK.

BACKSTONES BECK ROCK ART.

The rock art is one of the best on the moor. Its motif, a collection of interlocking lines and cup marks, shares parallels to the rock art of the North York Moors, particularly the Wainstones. Like the Wainstones, it would seem this area was used throughout prehistory, from the Neolithic through the Bronze Age. Environmental science has suggested this area was home to a small lake around 2500 BC. The discovery of Neolithic pits and tools, as well as possible Bronze Age structures, suggests Green Crag was an area of settlement.

The so-called Backstone Circle, on the other hand, is a crude fake. The feature, consisting of four stones, is situated within a sheep enclosure south of Ilkley Crags. South of this circle are another four upright stones – all unscathed by weathering. It has a confusing layout. Some have argued, unconvincingly, that there is a concentric stone circle here. That would be an important discovery, as only fifteen such monuments exist across England.

THE HAYSTACK ROCK

SE 13027 46314

This colossal haybale-shaped boulder lies south of Ilkley Crags, in an elevated position overlooking the east side of Ilkley. The rock has over seventy cup marks pecked into its surface, some surrounded by deep rings. Most of the art survives on top of the stone, on either side of a ridge that runs down its spine. The cups are clustered in parallel lines, often intersected by natural linear grooves in the stone. It seems the artist (or artists) used the natural shape of the rock to their advantage, framing the motifs between its striations.

Across from Haystack Rock is the Three Cups Stone, a small boulder displaying three wide cups. Some believe this to be a standing stone, carried and erected here. While this could be the case, there is currently no evidence for such a claim. The cup-marked face of the stone faces Haystack Rock, so it may be considered part of an alignment.

THE IDOL STONE

SE 13265 45946

The Idol Stone lies 400m from Haystacks Rock, beside the footpath leading towards High Lanshaw Dam. It sits in a well-trodden enclave from the surrounding heather, making locating it easy.

The motif is both typical of Yorkshire's cup and ring mark tradition, and distinct in its execution. Many parallel cup marks are surrounded by winding lines that were carved in rows, divided by carved grooves. These motifs, particularly the snaking lines, align with the boulder's shape, one surrounding the whole motif, the other encasing seven cups. While parallel cup marks and ring markings are found across northern Britain, linear carvings are far rarer. Ilkley Moor is one of the few regions where linear carvings survive in abundance.

One of the cup mark clusters is arranged in two parallel lines, four in each line. This is a common style of grouping cup marks, found repeatedly on Ilkley Moor. Since we can identify this specific pattern, we may be able to date the art. In the Lake District, similar motifs are commonly found in Neolithic contexts, near where stone tools were sourced and traded. If this carving is following the same tradition, we may date it to between 3800 BC and 3200 BC.

THE SKIRTFULS OF STONE

Two monuments on Ilkley Moor share the name Skirtful of Stones, a common moniker for large round cairns. They are both found alongside several ring cairns. Because ring cairns were frequently associated with cremations, we can assume they played a role in the Skirtfuls' ritualistic burials.

THE GREAT SKIRTFUL OF STONES, OVERLOOKING LEEDS TO THE SOUTH.

First, there is the **Great Skirtful of Stones** (SE 14056 44547), east of the Grubstones. It is monumental, but damaged. Most of the cairn's volume was quarried in the past, leaving only its outer edges. It is approximately 25m in diameter and would have stood at around 1.8m tall. It was once the largest and most important, and likely highest-status, burial monument on the moor. Trailing off to the immediate east of the barrow is a row of small ring cairns.

Second, and more impressive today, is the **Little Skirtful of Stones** (SE 13831 45190). 'Little' is wrong in this sense, as this cairn is immense. Like the Great Skirtful, it has been quarried in the past, so its original bowl shape has been lost. What we see today is the skeleton of the monument, stripped of its exterior and gnarled beyond recognition. Despite this, the sloppy autopsy revealed how large some of the stones used in its construction were. Many of these feature cup marks, suggesting Neolithic-carved rocks were used in their construction.

During the Early Bronze Age, Ilkley Moor underwent development as an agricultural landscape. The process of stone clearance would have taken place during this period, and we can safely assume that the stones moved from farmland ended up on burial cairns like the Little Skirtful. Reportedly, a map from the eighteenth century depicted the Little Skirtful surrounded by a stone circle, but today no such circle remains. Instead, only several prominent kerb stones are visible around the cairn.

BADGER/BARMISHAW/ PANORAMA/WILLY HALL'S WOODS STONES

The central hillside overlooking Ilkley may be the epicentre of UK rock art. Here you can find a vast assortment of complex rock carvings, featuring both well-known and wholly unique motifs. The four best examples lie north, south and inside of Willy Hall's Wood. These are the **Badger Stone**, the **Barmishaw Stone**, the **Panorama Stone** and the **Willy Hall's**

LEFT: WILLY HALL, RIGHT: BARMISHAW, TOP: BADGER.

Woods Stone (see back of book for grid references). Two unique motifs are found on these stones: a so-called ladder motif and a swastika. These may be multi-period carvings, featuring Neolithic, Bronze Age and Medieval designs.

BRADUP 'STONE CIRCLE' (LOST)

SE 08950 43900

Depending on who you ask, the story of Bradup Stone Circle is either one of the saddest in the annals of modern heritage preservation or a simple case of mistaken identity. It is not clear when this story starts, but our earliest reports of the site come courtesy of Robert Collyer, who in 1885 described a circle of eighteen large stones standing at the far south-west corner of Ilkley Moor. Following up on this, sometime before 1929, archaeologist Arthur Raistrick (explorer of Ox Close Stone Circle near Aysgarth and the Twelve Apostles) resurveyed the site, describing it as follows:

The circle ... has been very damaged at some period since 1885. At that date 18 stones were standing, but now only 12 remain, though there are large unfilled holes on the sites from which the other stones have been removed ... It seems certain that the stones were removed from this circle to repair the neighbouring Bradup Bridge, an act of vandalism always to be deplored ...

After Raistrick, accounts of the circle continued to show up in newspapers and gazetteers, all of which mentioned the sorry state the circle had been left in. According to local news articles, the circle had even been dubbed the 'Riddlesden Stonehenge'. In 1933, the site was given the honour of being listed as a scheduled monument, without a proper survey from an official body. This reckless decision resulted in the uncertain authenticity of Bradup Stone Circle and would come to curse it, as in 1994 it was abruptly descheduled after a surveyor from the Monuments Protection Programme (MPP) reported it to be nothing more than a natural spread of stones.

There were a few back-and-forth disagreements on the location of the circle described by Raistrick, but ultimately the site was deemed unworthy. Without any legal protection, the site would go on to vanish over the next ten years. Some speculated that the landowner, who had been assured the site was of no archaeological significance, had landscaped the field in which the circle sat, destroying it in the process. This, as is true for much of this story, is based on speculation.

There are arguments to be had from both sides. Some believe the MPP surveyor got it wrong, mistakenly surveying the adjacent field, thus causing Bradup's destruction, while others argue the surveyor got it right, and the landowner destroyed nothing of value in an empty field. Whatever the case, there is nothing to be found in either field today, and the question of whether this was, or was not, a prehistoric stone circle can no longer be answered for certain.

Author's note: The story of Bradup Stone Circle comes courtesy of Paul Bennet, who compiled an extensive history of the site on his website, The Northern Antiquarian.

BLACK HILL

Low Bradley Moor is a small patch of moorland south of Bradley. Perfect for a scenic stroll among fields of purple heather, this scrubby hillside is popular among local dog walkers. At its peak is Black Hill. Climbing the hill can take as little as twenty minutes, enjoyed in relative solitude. A perfect spot for the lazy romantic. Despite its modest appearance, Black Hill holds a treasure trove of prehistory, housing several rock art panels and burial monuments.

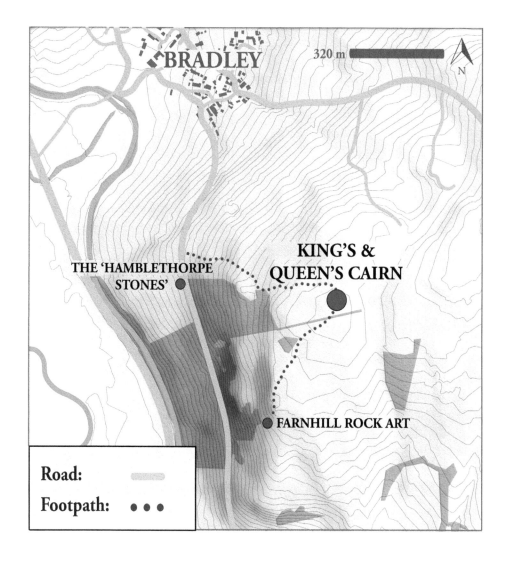

Low Bradley Moor sits at the tail end of two valleys, spanning between Kendal and Skipton; a beautiful place to get a bird's-eye view of the Southern Dales. Although it remains at a minor elevation compared to its neighbouring hills, the position of Low Bradley Moor is unmistakable. The 10km of lowlands between Skipton Moor and Kidstone Hill experience an abrupt halt with the appearance of Black Hill, rising defiantly from the heart of the Aire Valley. This commanding presence undoubtedly elevated the prestige of Black Hill, attracting the attention of Neolithic and Bronze Age elites, who sought to secure their final resting place upon its slopes.

KING'S CAIRN

SE 00924 47563

The King's Cairn is a much disturbed, yet significant, burial mound. It lies on the northern side of the moor, west of Tewit Mire Tarn. Venturing here is easy, and requires only a ten-minute walk, heading directly east from Crag Lane. Alternatively, if you are looking for more of a walk, you can head north from Kildwick, past the Farnhill Pinnacle, a cross celebrating Queen Victoria's Golden Jubilee.

The King's Cairn, which goes by several different names, is an example of an unchambered long cairn, an exceptionally rare style of burial monument, distinct from their better-known cousin, the long barrow. Like long barrows, long cairns date to the Early Neolithic period (est. 3500 BC). Unlike long barrows, long cairns rarely contain passages or chambers. Instead, like the round cairns of the Early Bronze Age, they usually contain multiple smaller cists (chambers are accessed from the side, while cists are sealed and only accessed from above).

Excavations in the early twentieth century removed its top, revealing its innards. Thanks to this, we can see its remarkable cist on full display. Archaeologists found multiple bodies within this cist, some as smashed bones, others as partial cremations. These bones were likely excarnated (their flesh was removed) prior to burial, as was typical of the Neolithic period. A 6ft-tall stone was also once present at the site, which stood atop the cairn. Such standing stones are often found among long cairns. Excavations in Cumbria and Oxfordshire, for instance, have shown evidence of stone and timber rows along the spines of long cairns.

But the story of the King's Cairn does not end in the Early Neolithic. Around a thousand years later, in the Early Bronze Age (est. 2300 BC), a massive round cairn was built on top of the long cairn. This was not an accident, but a motivated decision to build directly on top of an earlier grave. This clear layering of monuments is a blessing for archaeologists. Here, on full display, is a transparent demonstration of stratigraphy – a palimpsest of monuments. Obviously, we know the long cairn predated the round cairn because it sits below it.

THE CIST WITHIN THE KING'S CAIRN.

Why people chose to layer cairns over one another is not understood. Some speculate that layering was done in homage to the ancestors. Those buried within the long cairns were no doubt of high status. Combining your tomb with that of a powerful ancestor may have been an inexpensive way to enhance your burial. Similar examples of multi-period phases of burial are found at Raiset Pike Long Cairn in Cumbria and West Kennet Long Barrow near Avebury.

Author's note: Another theory contends that the Bronze Age act of building atop Neolithic barrows was a show of dominance. A huge cultural shift rocked the British Isles around 2500 BC. The introduction of the Bell Beaker culture coincided with a massive population decline among the already-dwindling Neolithic megalith builders. Round burial mounds started to appear around the same time.

The culture that built the long cairn would have been quite different to those who built the round cairn, with their own distinct languages, genealogies and values. Layering over prominent burial monuments may have been a way to architecturally display a takeover. There are more recent examples of cultural conversion via architectural dominance. The Mayan Pyramid of Cholula in Mexico, for instance, was adorned with a Spanish church. The Hagia Sophia in Istanbul was also converted to a mosque after the fall of Constantinople in 1453.

QUEEN'S CAIRN

SE 00873 47537

It is only fitting for the King's Cairn to have its Queen, and this one is big, round and ruinous. She appears to have had a rough 4,500 years.

She, or rather it, can be found directly to the south-west of the King's Cairn, aligned to the south-west, towards the setting of the winter solstice sun. It was built during the same period that the round cairn was added to the King's Long Cairn: the Early Bronze Age. In true Bronze Age fashion, it sits just before the apex of the moor, creating a false horizon, as the view beyond gives way to nothing but sky.

With 360-degree views on all sides, this is both a fantastic viewpoint and a prominent feature. It is like other upland cairns in the Yorkshire Dales, particularly Stoney Raise near Aysgarth. Unfortunately, like Stoney Raise, it was robbed in the past. Indeed, the wall that runs the length of Low Bradley Moor likely owes much to this cairn. However, on its northern edge is a ring cairn, hidden among the dense heather. This later addition may have been formed using stones robbed from the cairn, in a similar fashion to sites in the North York Moors (see Great Ayton Bank Cairn).

In the Dales, such large cairns are often found alone, on secluded moorlands or hilltops. Unlike the barrows found across the North York Moors, the Early Bronze Age round cairns of the west are far lonelier. In this respect, the cairns in the Yorkshire Dales are characteristically western, appearing more like burial monuments in Ireland, Wales and Cumbria. The Queen's Cairn and King's Cairn are exceptions to this. This is also true of the Skirtful cairns on Ilkley Moor. In all cases, later people noticed this, pairing them by name (Little Skirtful and Great Skirtful/King's Cairn and Queen's Cairn).

HAMBLETHORPE STONES

SE 00304 47627

The Hamblethorpe Stones are a proposed pair of standing stones in a field west of Crag Lane. It is easy to see the stones as they sit below the road, directly south of Bradley.

There is not much that can be said about these rocks, as there has been little investigation into their origins. Some have speculated that they represent a Neolithic monument, a short row known as a stone pair. While not common in Yorkshire, stone pairs are found in abundance in western England and Scotland. As the stones sit in the far west of Yorkshire, it is possible they follow the same tradition.

THE SO-CALLED HAMBLETHORPE STONES.

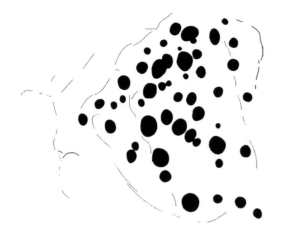

A SKETCH OF THE FARNHILL ROCK ART.

FARNHILL ROCK CANVAS

SE 00639 47104

South of the Farnhill Monument, which stands at the peak of the moor, you can find this lonely canvas of rock art. It is etched onto a sizable boulder on the edge of the slope towards Crag Lane. Like the other prehistoric sites around Black Hill, the Farnhill Rock Canvas is western in appearance. Unlike the intricate linear motifs found on Ilkley Moor, this canvas is a simple collection of deep cup marks. Motifs of this style (est. 3600–3200 BC) are found more frequently close to the Irish Sea, where ring marks are an uncommon feature.

FEIZOR THWAITE

The hamlet of Feizor, a sleepy little farming settlement at the far south-west of the Dales, is a popular spot for casual walkers. Its closeness to Pot Scar and Giggleswick Scar makes it ideal for low-intensity hiking, and the numerous small caves in the surrounding area are interesting to poke around in. However, given its location on the Dales' peripheries, off the A65 between Cumbria and Skipton, Feizor remains a well-kept secret.

Nevertheless, while the moors east of the hamlet are an excellent place to walk, they may be better recognised as an archaeological hotspot.

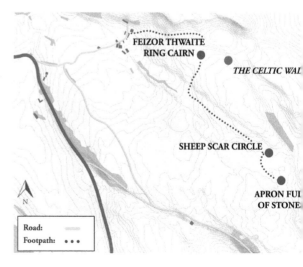

Feizor Thwaite Moor, which spans between Feizor to the west and Settle to the east, is densely scattered with prehistoric features. Most of these appear to be settlement remains as circular impressions found along the ridgeline are indicative of round houses. The caves, too, have been explored and found to have been used throughout prehistory. But, as it relates to this book, there is what seems to be a regional variety of kerbed ring cairn on Feizor Thwaite. Again, these remains are little explored, and badly catalogued; there is likely still much to be found on Feizor Thwaite.

APRONFUL OF STONES

SD 80653 66195

Not to be mistaken for the Apron Full of Stones (see 'Other Sites' in the Yorkshire Dales section), the Apronful of Stones survives beside a footpath running between Feizor and Stackhouse. It sits close to a quarry on a small knoll overlooking Studfold to the north. Finding it can be challenging on gloomier days as it blends in well with the piles of quarry waste in the same field. Look out for its distinctive capstone slab, strewn over its ruined cist.

THE APRONFUL'S INNARDS.

The Apron is massive, measuring 18m (59ft) in diameter and 1.5m (5ft) tall. Like other round cairns this large, the Apron dates to the Early Bronze Age. But like many cairns in the UK, it has been damaged by sloppy antiquarian investigations. The eighteenth-century *Gentleman's Magazine* detailed antiquarian plundering at the cairn. According to the magazine, up until excavation, the cairn had stood tall, with a megalithic kerb around its base and a flat top. Again, these details allude to the Apron's Bronze Age origins, likely closer to the earlier years of that period (est. 2500 BC).

During the excavation, several cists were reportedly discovered. Within these were 'several human bones scattered up and down therein', what is known as a disarticulated burial. Non-cremated skeletons, like those described, are usually either Neolithic or Early Bronze Age in date. Only a few of these cairns typically occupy an area and, unlike the round barrows of the east, Early Bronze Age cairns often stand alone, or in rare cases in pairs. In this case, there is an adjacent ring cairn, Sheep Scar Circle, where bodies were prepared for burial.

Early Bronze Age funerals seem to have involved alignments to the solstice sun, which can be witnessed here. Standing at the Apronful of Stones, looking towards Sheep Scar Circle, will align you towards the summer solstice sunset and, conversely, the winter solstice sunrise.

'APRON'-INSPIRED NAMES ORIGINATE FROM LOCAL FOLKLORE.

SHEEP SCAR CIRCLE

SD 80518 66477

Sheep Scar Circle lies next to a footpath north of the Apronful of Stones. It is one of two ring cairns hidden above Giggleswick Scar. The circle is made up of loose stones, forming an enclosure 10m across. A kerb bolsters its edges on either side, forming a thick band of stone. So-called kerbed ring cairns like this are typically Early Bronze Age, roughly dating between 2500 BC and 2000 BC.

SHEEP SCAR CIRCLE'S INNER CIST.

Within the embankment are the remains of a single burial cairn. Excavations in the eighteenth century damaged this cairn, leaving only the sunken cist we see today. According to the *Gentleman's Magazine*, the excavation revealed 'a skeleton, scattered human bones, an "ivory" disc, and a tusk'. These are now lost, so the nature of the enigmatic 'ivory disk' is sadly unknown. It is, however, unlikely an ivory artefact was unearthed here, and the item may have instead been either bone or walrus tusk.

In the early nineteenth century, Tot Lord, an archaeologist famed for his local cave excavations, excavated the site. Skeletal remains were found within the enclosure, alongside a Neolithic axe head. Further investigations took place in the 1960s. Flint tools were found inside the cist, and sherds of pottery dating to the Early Bronze Age were unearthed just outside. The sherds were found under where the cairn had stood over the cist, suggesting they predated it.

The excavations tell us several things. First, the cairn has strong ties to the Early Bronze Age, with disarticulated skeletons, broken pottery sherds and flint tools. Second, this was a site used for several centuries. Starting as an area for funerary rights, the enclosure was converted to a burial plot when a cairn and a cist were added. Multi-stage funerary enclosures like this are numerous across Britain, dubbed 'monuments in progress'. Similar kerbed circles are found to the west, in Lancashire and Cumbria, where excavations have unearthed evidence of the Beaker culture, some of the earliest Bronze Age settlers in Britain. This would suggest, through comparison alone, that Sheep Scar Circle was built towards the end of the Neolithic (est. 2500 BC).

CELTIC WALLS

SD 80086 67417

These bizarre structures are, potentially, the only Iron Age monuments listed in this book (not counting Skipsea Castle and Castle Dykes). They stand just east of Feizor Thwaite Ring Cairn, jutting up from a limestone pavement over-looking Stainforth. Despite their appeal, they are not mentioned on most maps. Thankfully, venturing to them is easy. Follow the main footpath east from the centre of Feizor, then adhere to the well-trodden track in the first field and continue up the hill to the north. The Celtic Walls are located on the edge of this hill, towards the limestone cliff face north of Dead Man's Cave.

Little research has been performed on these delicate structures, and there has been hesitation to call them prehistoric at all. After all, these are impressive prehistoric structures, and great claims require great evidence. Nevertheless, close inspection reveals quirks in what appears to be simple dry-stone walling. One cannot put into writing just how alien the Celtic Walls appear among the otherwise bleak moorland. Not only are they 5ft wide, but they are also formed with megalithic slabs of limestone. For reference, you can easily compare them to the nearby modern drystone walls to see the difference in size and weathering. It is stark.

The two 'walls' stand together, appearing as if they once formed a continuous tract. Originally, they were believed to be the unbroken remains of an Iron Age palisade wall (a non-surviving entity in England). However, the two sections appear to have been rounded off at their ends, suggesting they were never joined together. They seem to have been designed to stand as two individual structures, or potentially as monuments.

The secret to the Celtic Walls may lie directly beneath the ground. Under each wall sit elongated mounds, which terminate where the walls do. These unassuming lumps, which you may mistake for limestone pavement, were believed by some, including famed archaeologist Frank Elgee, to be burial

THE LARGEST OF THE CELTIC WALLS.

monuments. Indeed, sections of similar walling nearby were excavated in the early twentieth century, revealing Iron Age burials. Additionally, human remains belonging to five individuals were found in the adjacent field, along with several iron knives. This was a style of burial known as a 'clint burial', where people used natural seams in limestone as burial spaces. If the Celtic Walls were, as comparisons suggest, Iron Age burial spaces, they may represent a unique style of burial cairn localised to the area surrounding Settle.

Author's note: Of course, there are those who doubt the walls. As nice as it would be to gaze upon true Iron Age burial monuments, unique to the Dales, there is no proof the Celtic Walls are ancient. Just because some Iron Age burials have been discovered in similar locations does not prove anything. Although circumstantial evidence is the bread and butter of archaeology, it is usually drawn from a backlog of research.

GIGGLESWICK SCAR RING CAIRN

SD 79798 67471

This well-defined circle sits next to the main track over Feizor Thwaite Moor's central spur, to the west of the Celtic Walls. It is variously marked on maps as either an 'enclosure', a 'barrow' or not at all. Nevertheless, the site is wrongly scheduled as a stone circle, and therefore protected by law as such. Despite this, it is difficult to appreciate it from the ground. As such, it is recommended to either get an elevated view from Pot Scar opposite or have a look with a drone if one is available.

The feature consists of a thick embankment, which has become overgrown with long moorland grass. Like many slight circular features across the Dales, it is believed to be either a ring cairn, hut circle or cremation cemetery. We can easily dismiss the hut circle theory because there are no gaps in the embankment where a doorway could have stood. It is likely this was, like the Sheep Scar Circle, a kerbed ring cairn, used during funerals in the Early Bronze Age.

At its centre is a mound, or possibly a cairn. This may represent a burial or a robbed-out cist falling in on itself. Whatever the case, it again shares parallels to Sheep Scar Circle, which included an inner cist burial. A monument in progress, Feizor Thwaite Circle was likely used for several purposes over many generations. Starting as a cremation cemetery, where bodies were processed for burial, it was eventually retired, becoming a showy burial space.

Author's note: In 2023, an analysis was conducted on a skeleton discovered within a comparable ring cairn at Levens Park, Cumbria. The findings unveiled that these remains contained the earliest case of the plague (Yersinia pestis), in Britain. Interestingly, it appears the use of ring cairns coincided with the outbreak of a plague pandemic that spread throughout Europe.

OTHER SITES IN THE YORKSHIRE DALES/ WEST YORKSHIRE

APRON FULL OF STONES

SD 70915 78809

The Apron Full of Stones is a colossal pile of rocks positioned in Kingsdale between Gragareth and Stephenson's Hill. A modern retaining wall protects it from Long Gill, a winterbourne stream that flows below the cairn during rainy spells. It stands on private land, but you can view it from Thornton Lane, which runs parallel to the river.

THE APRON FULL OF STONES.

Most archaeological databases list the Apron as a ring cairn. While this could be argued, the cairn does not resemble one. If it were a ring cairn, the inner area would be traversable, like a stone circle or henge. Yet there is little symmetry to the Apron's current appearance. Therefore, we can assume its current shape is a result of robbing. The Apron is, in greater likelihood, a dilapidated round cairn, cut in two by Long Gill. Indeed, the western half of the Apron can be seen scattered across the river. If so, it once stood around 25m in diameter and over 8ft tall.

A 1972 excavation uncovered some tantalising artefacts. High-quality flints were unearthed, indicative of Neolithic activity. As round cairns like this typically date to the Bronze Age, the inclusion of stone age flints is curious. It may indicate the site was built in the transitional period between the use of stone and metal (i.e., the Early Bronze Age). Its size supports an Early Bronze Age date, as similar cairns often date between 2500 BC and 2000 BC. Early Bronze Age cists would have existed within its large mass. Containing full skeletons, these cists would also have included burial accessories, all of which were likely swept away by the river. Cremated remains were also discovered during the excavation. These were secondary burials, added in the middle Bronze Age.

SOLDIERS' TRENCH

SE 13052 39106

A mess of a site, known locally as the Soldiers' Trench, sprawls across Shipley Glen, to the immediate east of Bingley. Variously described as a stone circle, an Iron Age enclosure and a field system, the Soldiers' Trench is a warzone of conflicting opinions. Nevertheless, it appears to be nothing more than a natural spread of stones.

There are, however, some tangible pieces of prehistory to be had here. Several of the stones making up the jumble of rocks do exhibit Neolithic cup and ring motifs. This is not surprising, however, as the adjacent Baildon Moor is chock-full of Neolithic rock art. Certainly, of all the examples to focus on nearby, those on Shipley Glen are some of the least interesting.

HARE HILL RING CAIRN

SD 92954 47698

The Hare Hill Ring Cairn sits 4km from Barnoldswick, on Thornton Moor. It is a small (17m across) example of a kerbed ring cairn, a style of enclosure common in Lancashire and South Lakeland. Such monuments have megalithic stones surrounding a circular rubble bank, holding it neatly in place. They are typical of the Early Bronze Age Beaker People, and excavations at this example did unearth pottery and jewellery typical of that culture.

WEST AGRA ROCK ART

SE 14239 81749

The carvings at West Agra, found on several rocks to the south of the West Agra forestry plantation, are among the best in Yorkshire. They were rediscovered in 2003 and since then five rock art panels have been identified in the immediate area.

The carvings range from clusters of cups to linear lines and rings. They are like the carvings at Ilkley, especially those on the Willy Hall's Wood Stone and the Idol Stone. Of the collection, a cup and ring mark within the plantation are standouts. This motif is well preserved, exhibiting a similar ladder motif seen repeatedly on Ilkley Moor, replacing the more common tail that runs through many ring markings.

A SKETCH OF ONE OF THE WEST AGRA ROCK ART MOTIFS.

EWDEN BECK

SK 23810 96640

Nestled amidst the rolling hills of the eastern reaches of the Peak District lies a small and mysterious ring cairn. It sits just north-east of the hamlet of Wigtwizzle. Little is known of the ancient monuments that dot the South Yorkshire landscape, and this circle is one of the few that have been uncovered. The hilltop upon which it stands is rich in archaeology, surrounded by Bronze Age dykes and dotted with burial mounds. Supposedly, a polished stone axe was discovered within one of these barrows in the late nineteenth century, though some say it may have been found within the ring cairn itself.

THE TODMORDEN MONOLITHS

SD 92521 23598

The Todmorden Monoliths are situated neither in the Yorkshire Dales nor in the historic county of Yorkshire. They are, therefore, making only a cameo appearance in the form of this small mention at the end of the chapter. Antiquarians often included these stones, using the name Bride-Stones, when cataloguing West Yorkshire's prehistoric sites. The site was described in 1822 by Thomas Langdale, but it is unclear whether he ever visited the site himself. He wrote:

> *In Stansfield, are many Druidical places of worship, such as Hawkstones, Bride-stones ... the last consists of one upright stone or pillar, called the Bride, whose perpendicular height is about five yards; near this stood another large stone, called the Groom, which is now thrown down by the country people; and at small distances several others ... so scattered about the common, that at first view, the whole looks something like a temple of the serpentine kind.*

As with the Bridestones near Grosmont (see Chapter 1), it appears that there was more to the Todmorden Monoliths than meets the eye. It seems one of the stones, likely the northern one (now shaped and embedded in a pedestal on the hill), was once laid beside the larger stone near the road. However, the other stones mentioned, which may have formed a stone row, no longer survive.

TURTLEY HOLES STONES

SD 99833 22367

Over Withers Moor, to the east of the Todmorden Stones, you can find another possible collection of standing stones known as the Turtley Holes Stones. First mentioned in 2006 by Dr D. Shepherd on the internet forum Megalithic Portal, there are at least two likely prehistoric standing stones in the collection. They are outliers, sitting only 10 miles (20km) from Greater Manchester. Therefore, like the Todmorden Stones, these would fit better into an investigation of north-western prehistoric sites.

BAILDON MOOR (LOST)

The rock art on Baildon Moor is equal in quality to that of Ilkley Moor. With only a shallow valley separating the two, between the north and south, they could be considered part of the same collection. On this tract of land, stretching a single mile, you can find over forty stones adorned with Neolithic carvings. One of the finest examples of rock art here lies within Dobrudden Caravan Park. The Dobrudden Stone, as it is known, is cemented into the wall on the north side of the caravan park. It features twenty-six cups across its face, arranged in parallel lines, between which several linear carvings snake and twist.

Among this collection of rock art was the now lost Dobrudden Necropolis. This was described by antiquarian J.N.M. Colls in the mid-nineteenth century, along with several large circular earthworks, possibly henges, and the remains of an urn. Colls also described finding numerous linear embankments that may have represented a prehistoric field system, likely of the Bronze or Iron Age. Colls' investigation was among the first to describe cup and ring marks in England, but with a sceptical mind he was hesitant to attribute them to artists. He stated in his 1845 report:

some of the stones of which they and the earthworks near them were constructed, had marks, or characters, but so rude that a doubt remains whether they may not have been caused by the action of the atmosphere on the softer portions of the stone.

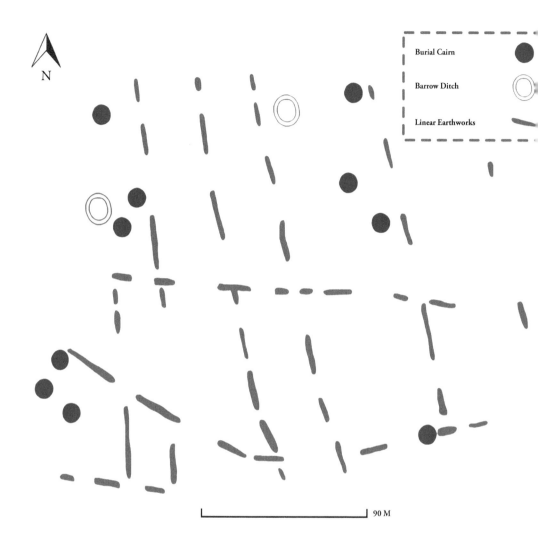

90 M

THE DOBRUDDEN NECROPOLIS, BASED ON A SKETCH BY J.N.M. COLLS.

Colls also described several stone circles on the moor, including a rare concentric circle. Such circles comprise two or more rings of stone arranged inside one another, usually with a burial at their centre. He described it as two circles, having an outer circle of eighteen stones and an interior circle of six. Colls' circle, on the other hand, could be interpreted as the remains of a kerbed ring cairn, which have often been mistaken for concentric stone circles.

Most of these features were lost without further study. It would seem the cairns and stone circles were quarried for building material and the earthworks ploughed away. In modern times, rescue excavations would have been carried out long before any development took place, with plans and finds recorded in a database. In fact, no developments, especially not quarrying, would have been allowed on such an important prehistoric landscape.

BROWN HILLS BECK TUMULI

SD 75640 60241

Like the Todmorden Monoliths, these massive round barrows are outliers, sitting just over the county border in Lancashire. Although rarely discussed, especially in books on Yorkshire, the Brown Hills Beck Tumuli are Yorkshire monuments in all but their situation. They are found over 4km (2.7 miles) from the nearest public roads, in the centre of Gisburn Forest, so access is difficult.

Together with their near perfect level of preservation, these barrows are massive – ranking among the tallest examples in Yorkshire and easily qualifying as the tallest barrows in Lancashire. They stand 8m (26ft) and 10m (32ft) tall. Little research has been performed on the mounds, but it would seem they share similarities with barrows in the Vale of Mowbray and East Riding. Morphologically (judging by the way they look), it would seem they are either Neolithic or Early Bronze Age in origin.

HARDEN MOOR STONE CIRCLE

SE 07497 38678

It feels like a shame to relegate this little circle to the end of this chapter. However, despite being found just north of Bradford, it sits further south than any other site listed in this book, making it isolated in comparison. You can easily access it via the many well-trodden footpaths across Harden Moor. Recent restoration work on the moor (in 2021) has exposed the circle for the first time in millennia, revealing a site almost too perfect to believe.

HARDEN MOOR STONE CIRCLE AND WILSDEN.

It is a six-and-a-half-metre wide enclosure of stone, composed of at least 24 megaliths. At its centre is a small traversable area, just big enough to congregate inside with several people. It is likely the surviving kerb of a long-lost burial mound, but some believe it to be an embanked stone circle (a type of ring cairn). This is evident in stones' proximity to one another, the lack of an obvious ring cairn beneath them, and the site's location just below the brow of the hill. Like most kerbed barrows, it dates to the Early Bronze Age, as numerous excavations have found both Neolithic artefacts (including a cup marked stone) and Bronze Age pottery within its centre. Numerous post holes have been found in and around the site, though what they represent remains debatable.

COTTINGLEY WOODS

SE 09773 37857

The area surrounding Bradford is home to a host of surviving prehistoric sites. To the south-east of Harden Moor, in Cottingley Woods, an extraordinary collection of rock art survives. These motifs, which are like those on the nearby Ilkley Moor, are clustered around the west end of the Blackhills Campsite, on private land. Again, as the area is something of an archaeological black hole, hidden from interested eyes, there has been little work performed to help contextualise the archaeology. If you are willing to risk the fairies, Cottingley Wood would be a good spot to search for undiscovered rock art.

COTTINGLEY WOOD'S UNUSUAL ROCK ART.

THE TREE OF LIFE

SE 18016 50603

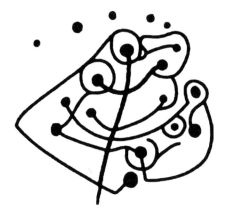

A SKETCH OF THE TREE OF LIFE.

Arguably the most impressive rock art site in Yorkshire, the so-called Tree of Life lies on the eastern edge of Snowden Carr, to the north-east of Ilkley. It looks like a tree, although this is most likely a coincidence. Neolithic/Bronze Age rock art is very rarely figurative. However, a similar carving lies 12km north, in Guisecliff Woods, suggesting the motif was more widespread.

CHAPTER FOUR

EAST RIDING –
THE YORKSHIRE WOLDS

We end this journey with, arguably, Yorkshire's most important prehistoric landscape. Nowhere listed in this book is as enigmatic as East Riding, a region whose archaeology speaks of ritual activity dating as far back as the Mesolithic period (8000–4000 BC). While much of this is only evident in the form of artefacts (many now taking prime positions at the British Museum), there remain several Neolithic and Bronze Age monuments surviving in the landscape, as impressive as they are curious.

East Riding seems to have been an area with extensive connections to other regions of Britain. One of the ways we know this is by the sheer number of artefacts found here that originate from far away. Polished stone axes are the most striking examples of this phenomenon. Axe heads originating from Cornwall, and even Ireland, have been ploughed up over the years, likely having been inserted into later burial mounds as votive offerings. However, by far the biggest connection seems to have been to the Lake District in Cumbria. Dozens, if not hundreds, of polished axe heads originating from the so-called 'Langdale Axe Factory' have been unearthed in East Riding. East Riding has the most Langdale axe heads discovered in Britain, even more than Langdale itself. Cumbria, Cornwall and Ireland share many similarities in Neolithic culture, and this connection may imply a relationship between the Western British Neolithic culture (est. 3800–2800 BC) and the monuments of East Riding.

East Riding also contains an astonishing number of burial mounds, comparable to Wiltshire, the home of Stonehenge. Almost every field has its own barrow. The majority have been destroyed by generations of ploughing, but thanks to the area's crop fields, satellite imagery is enough to see partial outlines via crop marks. As there are so many examples, we cannot possibly cover them all in this book. Therefore, this chapter will only detail the best surviving, which, thankfully, are among the most impressive in Europe.

While most of the sites listed in this book exist within the northern half of East Riding, there appears to have been a flourishing culture of monument building in the south, too. As recently as 2017, details of a timber circle within a henge monument at Little Catwick, Hornsea, were published. It would seem the Neolithic culture of henge building spread widely from the Vale of Mowbray, through Catterick, Thornborough and Rudston, all the way down to Hull. Indeed, while variations in monument styles occurred between regions, there remains a through-line between them all: their shared roots in the Neolithic and their fascination with the sky.

The sky here is vast and sprawling, a canvas often painted with endless shades of blue, grey and gold. On clear days, you can see the curvature of the earth in the distance, a reminder of the great mystery of the cosmos. At night, the stars twinkle brightly, a timeless and ethereal sight that brings one to a place of quiet contemplation. It is no wonder, then, that Neolithic people flocked to East Riding for religious ceremonies.

RUDSTON

When you enter a village whose name alludes to the word 'stone', there is little doubt megaliths are nearby. In this case, the name Rudston derives from Old English. 'Rud' derivates from the word 'rood', meaning 'cross', and 'ston' derivates from 'stone'. When taken literally, Rudston translates to 'cross stone'.

For anyone interested in megalithic monuments across Europe, this should be no surprise, because Rudston, in all its unassuming quaintness, holds the tallest standing stone in Britain. Once topped by a cross in the medieval period, the Rudston Monolith stands in the graveyard of All Saints Church. The church, dating to the Norman Conquest, was built beside the megalith. From there, the surrounding village grew. You can also find a smaller standing stone in the north-eastern corner of the churchyard, alongside the remains of two cists. These were moved here in 1869 after being taken from a barrow on Rudston Beacon to the south.

Stones so large do not appear out of the blue. You would expect such a large monument to be surrounded by ruins and tombs, like the more famous Stonehenge. Yet in Rudston, little remains visible from ground level. However, dig a little deeper and a wildly different story emerges. Under the village's red-brick houses lie some of northern England's largest, and oldest, earthworks. Four cursus monuments, two standing stones, a rare Neolithic settlement and a small canvas of rock art have been discovered in and around Rudston.

Ploughed flat over the centuries, Rudston's prehistory only reveals itself on rare occasions: when it is hot. Given the right conditions, shallow crop soils dry out, revealing where trenches were once dug into the bedrock. Using aerial imagery, researchers have shown Rudston to have been a hotbed of prehistoric activity.

Among the earliest features in the area are the lost Rudston, Denby and Kilham long barrows, to the west of Rudston, dating between 3600–3200 BC. The Kilham Long Barrow, south of Dotterill Park, was twice excavated, once by William Greenwell, and again by T.G. Manby. Activity at Kilham began with the construction of an enclosure with an outer palisade, alongside several timber buildings. The long barrow was then built directly on top of these features, and used throughout the Early Neolithic. Later, in the Bronze Age, offerings were planted in the barrow, including several cremations and beakers.

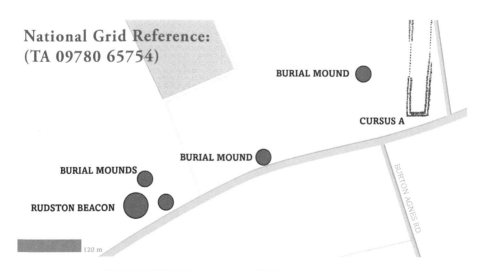

THE LOST PREHISTORIC LANDSCAPE ON RUDSTON BEACON.

THE RUDSTON BEACON CIST IN THE GRAVEYARD OF ALL SAINTS CHURCH.

After the long barrows, the chronology of Rudston gets muddy. We do know several earthworks, such as henges and cursus monuments, were constructed between 3500 BC and 3200 BC. Later, around 3000 BC, several massive barrows were built, such as Southside Mount. There seems to have been non-stop activity in the region, with one major lull around the mid-Bronze Age. Once the Roman period emerged at Rudston, activity again boomed, with several villas, settlements and temples being built in the area. When the Anglo-Saxons arrived, funerary activity at the Neolithic burial mounds continued throughout the region.

THE RUDSTON CURSUS GROUP

While best known for its standing stone, Rudston should equally be recognised for its earthworks. Known as the Rudston Group, the earthworks are now only visible as faint lines in crop fields. But while inconspicuous from ground level, these cursus monuments are precious beyond belief.

John Hedges and David Buckley once described cursus monuments as 'the most enigmatic of all known forms of earlier prehistoric earthworks in the British Isles'. Cursus monuments are among the oldest and rarest earthworks in Britain. They are cigar-shaped enclosures that snake through the landscape. Sometimes they extend less than the length of a modern field. In other instances, however, they cover vast swaths of land. The Dorset Cursus, for example, stretches more than 9km across the Dorset landscape. It is evident that cursus earthworks were important, as they are often found in areas of intense ritual activity. Such areas include Stonehenge, Newgrange and the Thornborough Henges. They are only known to exist in Britain, and while examples have been found in Scotland and Ireland, the majority are in southern England.

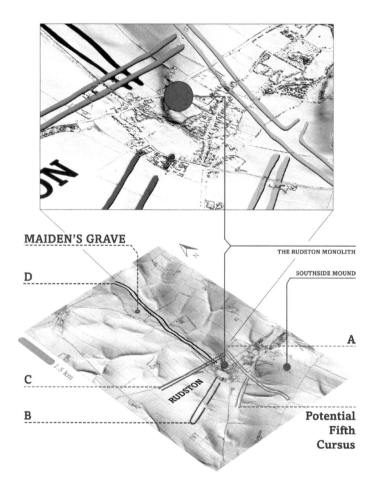

MAIDEN'S GRAVE

THE RUDSTON MONOLITH

SOUTHSIDE MOUND

D

A

C

B

RUDSTON

1.5 km

Potential
Fifth
Cursus

A MAP OF
THE CURSUS
MONUMENTS
AT RUDSTON.

Typically dating between 3800 BC and 3500 BC, they are among the oldest monuments in Britain. By the time the great sarsen stones were erected at Stonehenge, the adjacent cursus was already 700 years old. While they often exist near Neolithic stone monuments, they often predate them by at least several centuries. Indeed, if their extreme age is perplexing, their function is even more so. Roy Loveday, one of Britain's leading experts on cursus monuments, has described them as 'vast empty enclosures, often laid out with striking precision'. As described, most cursus monuments in England are devoid of internal features. Unlike later Neolithic monuments, which often align towards the solstices, cursus monuments demonstrate little pattern.

Rudston and its monuments represent an important link between cursus enclosures and the later standing stone/henge tradition. An astonishing five cursus monuments stood within a 3-mile radius of the Rudston Monolith: the highest concentration in England. They are labelled from **Rudston A** to **Rudston E**. The earthworks appear to criss-cross around the monolith, which is marked by a prominent bend in the Gypsey Race River, near the village centre. Additionally, to the north, a henge known as **Maiden's Grave** lies between Rudston D and the Gypsey Race.

There have been numerous surveys and excavations at the earthworks. Most attention has been given to Cursus A, south of Rudston. It weaves in a north–south alignment past Southside Mount in a dog's leg shape, terminating at the road towards Burton Agnes. It is thought to be the oldest cursus of the group, as Cursus C terminates before hitting it, as if to avoid intersecting. Its southern terminal is the only preserved portion of the Rudston Group, which caps off its 2½km span with a straight 90-degree trench (TA 09981 65810).

William Greenwell was the first to excavate this terminal in the mid-nineteenth century. He uncovered a round barrow, inside of which he found six burials. Only one of these dated to the Neolithic, while the other five were Early Bronze Age. In 1955, a second excavation unearthed a jumble of Beaker pottery from the ditch's bottom. This suggests the cursus was recut for ritual deposits during the Early Bronze Age. There are several more Bronze Age barrows east of the terminal. These sit next to another uncommon slice of archaeology: an Early Neolithic settlement, dating to around 3500 BC. Such settlement sites are rare. Indeed, despite the common belief that the Neolithic brought permanent settlements to all corners of Britain, people remained largely mobile until the mid-Bronze Age.

ONE OF THE CROPMARK SETTLEMENTS AT RUDSTON, INCORPORATING A SECTION OF CURSUS A.

Cursus A

Later Settlement

80 m

N

The largest of the four is Cursus D, which runs the length of the Gypsey Race. Cursus C intersects Cursus D, and excavations at this junction demonstrated that Cursus D is the youngest of the group. Beginning near Burton Fleming, it meanders south. It is the gnarliest of the four, having ditches only roughly parallel to one another. So far, no terminal has been revealed at its southern end, but it seems to have either terminated at the Rudston Monolith or took a sharp west turn, joining Cursus B.

Despite what we do know, cursus monuments remain among Britain's most enigmatic monuments. Theories on their purpose are varied. Some believe them to have been agricultural enclosures. Others believe them to have been complex religious enclosures. They may have been a little bit of both. Some archaeologists, such as Christopher Tilley, believe cursus monuments were designed to be walked down in a specific direction, acting like a well-planned sightseeing tour through the landscape. Within East Riding's undulating hills, where small dips can block substantial portions of the landscape, such a theory may be credible.

Henry Chapman, known for his surveying expertise on *Time Team*, used digital maps to examine the Rudston Cursus Group, exploring Tilly's idea of a sightseeing procession within the monuments. He found that Cursus A and C demonstrated 'directionality', where for those walking the length of the cursus, prominent natural features would come into view, one after the other. The later Cursus D, however, appears to have simply followed the Gypsey Race – aligning itself to the landscape's natural contours. The reasons for this are unknown, but it would seem that by the mid to late Neolithic, the focus of ceremonial enclosures had begun to shift.

In Rudston's case, there remains one big question: the monolith. How did this extraordinary megalith tie together with the earthworks? And why?

Author's note: To create the diagrams provided, I have traced numerous satellite images, ranging from 2004 to 2020. But there are still many gaps. Because most of the earthworks have no visible terminal, we do not know how long they stretched. A heatwave in 2018 provided the best conditions to see the crop marks yet. Scanning over the fields, a whole other world is revealed. Iron Age villages, Roman farms and Neolithic earthworks decorate the fields. It appears that people later converted the cursus trenches for their own purposes. Cursus A, for instance, has been redirected to surround a Roman-era settlement. This is as good as it gets without excavating; a bird's-eye map of an ancient landscape in full view.

THE RUDSTON MONOLITH –

TA 09805 67744

The Rudston Monolith is not only the tallest standing stone in Britain, but also one of the most fascinating. The stone stands in the graveyard of All Saints Church, Rudston. You can park anywhere in the village and walk right up to the stone with ease. It is hard to miss – and not just because it is well signposted: it stands 8m (25ft) tall and weighs a mighty 30 tons.

Erecting such a megalith would be challenging, especially during prehistory. Yet, compared to the story of its sourcing, this was only a meagre feat.

THE RUDSTON MONOLITH.

Neolithic people sourced the stone from the Cleveland Hills in the North York Moors, over 64km away from Rudston. More specifically, some believe the stone travelled from the moorlands surrounding Grosmont. If this were the case, then Neolithic monuments in that area, such as the High Bridestones, could be connected – in spirit – to the Rudston Monolith.

Given its proximity to the Neolithic earthworks around Rudston, it is tempting to suggest the stone also dates to that period. After all, Europe's most impressive standing stones tend to date to early periods. In France, for instance, stones of a comparable size date to the mid-fourth millennium BC (est. 3500 BC). Comparisons can also be drawn to the French standing stones of Champ-Dolent and Er Grah, which were sculpted, or 'dressed', to shape. The Rudston Monolith was likewise dressed, its sides smoothed and squared off. If we work from these comparisons, we can estimate the stone was erected during the Neolithic period: sometime between 3800 BC and 3000 BC. However, both the size and dressing of the monolith are also similar to the sarsens at Stonehenge, which date to the Early Bronze Age (est. 2500 BC). Therefore, we must concede that the stone remains undated by comparison alone.

To understand this megalith, we must first understand the landscape in which it stands. Most importantly, we must recognise its position among Rudston's cursus monuments.

The megalith stands where Cursus B and D converge, at the south end of Cursus D. Like most cursus earthworks, Cursus D does not share any alignments with the sun. Instead, it aligns roughly south, running from Burton Fleming to All Saints Church, following a uniquely north–south aligned stretch of the Gypsey Race. If the monolith stood within Cursus D, it may have acted like the sights on a rifle, aligning the cursus south. If so, why would such a large complex align to the south?

Cursus B terminates at a dramatic L-shaped bend in the Gypsey Race, which flows only 200m from the monolith. While this beck is unassuming at first glance, it is a rarity in the Yorkshire Wolds, a landscape with very few rivers. It is also a winterbourne stream, a river system that only flows during the winter months when springs open after consistent rainfall. Indeed, only a trickle of water flows through the Gypsey Race, and you can find it almost dry mid-summer. This makes the Gypsey Race something of a natural calendar, indicating the start of winter when water emerges. Even today,

witnessing water flowing through the Gypsey Race is a good indication that winter is fast approaching. Therefore, a processional path south, towards the Gypsey Race, may have made sense during winter, when water flowed past the south end of the cursus.

Imagine, if you will, a crisp winter morning. The sun has begun to bleed into the sky. Birds chirp and flutter between trees and fields, leaving trails in the frost as they go. It is the day of a festival, and you stand at the end of a great earthwork. You have come from far away, requiring several days of boating and a long trek north through thick forest. Your village elder, who studies the night sky, has foretold that celebrations will be held here in accordance with the stars. He and other religious leaders, each representing communities in your area, lead you and a crowd of hundreds down the centre of the cursus.

In the far distance, you can see it. While it is only a speck on the horizon now, you have been told of its magnitude. You and your village know exactly what it represents: the culmination of hard labour. In times long ago, your ancestors made the same pilgrimage to help haul the stone into place.

But, of course, this is all conjecture. Nobody knows, or will likely ever know, what gods, or god, if any, Neolithic people worshipped. Or, indeed, how they worshipped them. Theories on why, exactly, the stone stands at Rudston, do not help us understand why it had to be so large. However, there are several theories on why the erection of massive stones was useful to Neolithic communities.

First, the Rudston Monolith embellished Rudston's vast ceremonial landscape. By lifting such awe-inspiring stones, the area gained prestige, and the labour force would have been bolstered around a mega-project. People came from far and wide to help build Stonehenge, as they likewise did at Rudston. It was collaboration that allowed farming to develop in Britain, and collaboration that would result in monument construction.

Second, later generations may have paid homage to their ancestors' mega-constructions. Such homage is still seen today at holy sites, from the Western Wall in Jerusalem to the Masjid al-Haram in Mecca. Popular pilgrimage sites naturally spring up around impressive feats of lifting. By building big, you outwardly express your devotion to your god, in a way that stands the test of time.

Third, if the Neolithic era had dynastic leadership, those in charge of these complex engineering feats may have wished to demonstrate their immense power. Like the Pyramids of Giza or the empty skyscrapers of communist North Korea, authoritarian leaders often feel it necessary to flex their control via mega-constructions. In this case, encouraging a community to drag a 30-ton stone over 65km would no doubt promote loyalty to those who commissioned such extraordinary feats.

THE GREAT MOUNDS OF YORKSHIRE

A good portion of the Gypsey Race runs west to east, hugging the road between Duggleby and Burton Fleming. For much of its 22km length, this river appears to be nothing more than an overgrown hedgerow in the landscape. However, following its course, between Duggleby and Rudston, it serves as a guideline between some of Britain's grandest burial mounds. These Great Mounds, as they have come to be known, have yielded some of the richest prehistoric grave goods in Europe. On average, they stood around 8m tall and 30m in diameter, but the ravages of history have shortened them somewhat.

There are only four canonical Great Mounds in East Riding: **Southside Mount**, **Willie Howe**, **Duggleby Howe** and **Wold Newton**. However, these are not the only large and important barrows in the region. Therefore, I will be adding a few extra mounds to this category: the **Folkton Drums Barrow** and **Fox Hill**. There are also several monuments next to the mounds that have only survived as crop marks. Crop marks are especially prevalent in the Wolds, where the rich soils allow for remarkable clarity. On hot summer days, thousands of ghostly shapes emerge across the region's crop fields, the majority of which are the remains of Neolithic and Bronze Age burial mounds.

A vast amount of information on these mounds comes courtesy of antiquarian William Greenwell. His 1890 article, 'Recent Excavations in Yorkshire, Wiltshire, Berkshire' detailed his numerous excavations across England. Originally published in the journal *Archeologia*, this article detailed some of

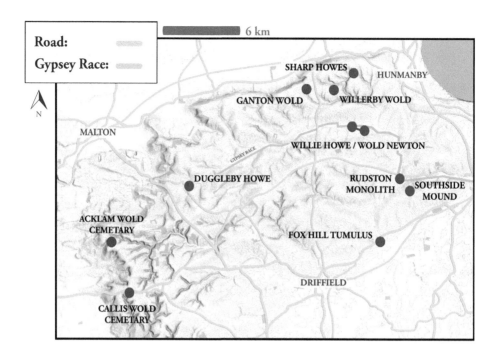

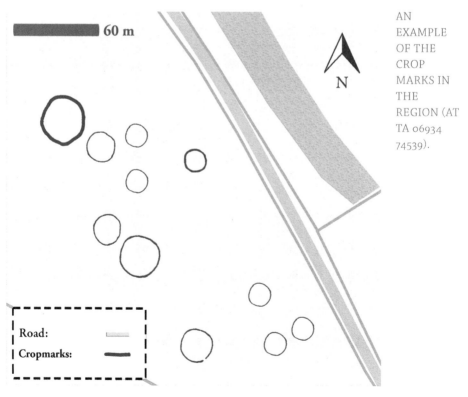

AN EXAMPLE OF THE CROP MARKS IN THE REGION (AT TA 06934 74539).

the finest prehistoric artefacts ever to have been discovered in Britain. Indeed, if you visit museums featuring prehistoric pottery, jewellery or weapons, many fine examples may be the result of Greenwell's excavations. Sadly, this came at a cost. Greenwell, as you may have gathered from other entries in this book, is to blame for the destruction and disfigurement of numerous burial mounds across Yorkshire.

SOUTHSIDE MOUNT

TA 10756 66580

Despite appearing as nothing more than a slight bump, Southside Mount is one of the four canonical Great Mounds of Yorkshire. It does not look impressive. But sitting within the ritual landscape at Rudston, east of the cursus, this barrow is among the most important in Yorkshire. A nearby footpath to the west provides a view of it.

Only one other mound survives within a mile of the Rudston Monolith, which sits in the forests south of the village. However, Southside Mount dwarfs this, being over 20m wider in diameter, and standing on a prominent spur overlooking Rudston. It would originally have stood around 9m tall and 90m in diameter. Around its base are the faint remains of a concentric ditch. Known as a quarry trench, the ditch was dug fist, and the earth and rubble thrown inwards to form the mound.

Although it may look like an Early Bronze Age burial mound, people formed Southside Mount over centuries, starting in the middle Neolithic era (est. at 3200 BC). At the end of the nineteenth century, Greenwell excavated Southside Mount and found that it consisted of several layers. During his excavation, he discovered a total of twenty-three burials, which were added in three stages over the course of 4,000 years. Below, I will provide details about these burials in reverse chronological order.

In **Stage Three**, the Anglo-Saxons reused the youngest section of the barrow. They buried a group of five men on their backs at the top of the mound, crossing their arms in Saxon fashion. These burial practices bear a striking resemblance to those found at Pudding Pie Hill (see Chapter 2), which the Saxons also altered.

In **Stage Two**, Greenwell discovered several crouched burials while digging deeper within the mound. These bodies, likely from the Early Bronze Age period, were sorted into individual graves, including a woman in a wood-lined grave and a young girl in a cist. Additionally, the graves contained charcoal, animal bones, Bronze Age pottery and flint tools.

In **Stage One** Greenwell uncovered a shaft beneath the mound. He found two bodies within this shaft – an infant and an adult female (possibly the mother). He also found leaf-shaped arrowheads typical of the Neolithic period placed beside the bodies. Although most of the mound is younger than Rudston Cursus C, it was evident that the site had been established during the mid-Neolithic era (est. 3200 BC). There was likely a monument in place before the shaft, possibly a smaller barrow, a timber circle or an enclosure of some variety.

Author's note: While extraordinary, Southside Mount is far from a lonely monument. Though now ploughed away, there was once a diverse collection of barrows on Rudston Beacon, the low hill to the south of Rudston. Some of these lost barrows are almost twice the size of Southside, alluding to an even grander funerary landscape in this area than we see today.

DUGGLEBY HOWE

SE 88051 66893

Duggleby Howe is the most north-westerly of Yorkshire's Great Mounds and is the best recognised of the four. It stands in a private field south-east of the village of Duggleby. It is easy to view, as you can see it from any of the adjacent roads. The best view is from Backside Lane to the north of the barrow.

If you are going to visit or study any of the Great Mounds of Yorkshire, Duggleby Howe should be your first choice. It is massive, at 6m high and 40m wide, with an estimated weight of 5,000 tons. It is also well preserved, standing proud within the landscape without any tree cover. It sits on the lower side of a hill, sitting near the bottom of the valley to the north. If you know anything about the position of burial mounds, this fact should perk your curiosity. This is because Bronze Age burial mounds are more often found on the tops of hills or near their crests – not within valleys.

The only damage to Duggleby Howe appears to be a result of an excavation by John Robert Mortimer in 1890; an excavation that found wonderful things.

Mortimer divided the mound's chronology into five phases, which he published in his 1905 book *Forty Years Researches in British and Saxon Burial Mounds of East Yorkshire*. These phases are chronologically as follows:

Phase 1 consisted of a single crouched inhumation of an adult male, buried in a wooden coffin within a shaft at the base of the mound. This man, presumably someone of importance, had several flint cores and a Towthorpe Bowl buried with him. A flint core is a large piece of worked flint, flaked into smaller pieces to fashion into tools. A Towthorpe Bowl is a rare style of Neolithic pottery, unique to north-east England. Such bowls are plain and rounded, with a big out-turned rim. There was no barrow in this early phase, which researchers date to around 3500 BC, during the Early Neolithic period.

Mortimer unearthed two more full skeletons above this man, one belonging to an adult and the other to an infant. Interestingly, the skull of the adult had been punctured with a sharpened club before death. There are several theories as to what this represents, but the reason that first jumps to mind is a grisly one: human sacrifice. This is not normal, and although Duggleby Howe is not necessarily unique in form, this discovery is rare.

In **Phase 2**, Neolithic people backfilled the shaft, and placed another two bodies upon the fill, becoming shallowly buried. They placed two artefacts alongside these bodies: a deer antler mace head and a stone axe, polished only on one end. A collection of unusual yet intricate grave goods dating to the Neolithic period.

Phase 3 saw the addition of a second shaft next to the first, this one shallow. An adult was placed into this, alongside a collection of arrowheads, some beaver teeth, boar's tusks and a bone hair pin. On the ground surface between the first shaft and the second, yet another skeleton was laid. Mortimer found an exquisite flint knife next to the skeleton, which had been knapped and polished to be only 1.5mm thick.

On top of this adult, the first evidence of a round barrow appeared, covering both this body, as well as the earlier shafts. Within this initial mound, the bones of four infants, three children, a teenager and one adult were placed. This phase is believed to have occurred between 2800 BC and 2700 BC, close to the Early Bronze Age and the subsequent arrival of the Beaker People.

Phase 4 likely occurred during the Early Bronze Age. During this time, over fifty cremated remains were inserted into the mound. These were not placed in urns before burial, but were rather scattered on the mound. So many ashes were scattered here, they formed an identifiable layer in the mound. Since Mortimer was unable to excavate all the mound without destroying it, it is likely many cremations in the mound were left undiscovered. The number of cremations scattered here may have exceeded 100.

Phase 5, the final phase of use at the mound saw the barrow grow to its current size. This was achieved by piling tonnes of quarried chalk over the original small mound. No burials were found within this phase, suggesting it did not serve a funerary function. Instead, this phase may be compared to Willy Howe (detailed in the next entry) and Silbury Hill, near Avebury. Such mounds would not have a practical function, but instead serve as 'cenotaphs'; erected to honour the dead, not hold them.

One of the most intriguing aspects of the Great Mounds, especially in the case of Duggleby Howe, is the presence of rich Neolithic grave goods. While grave goods from the Stone Age survive across Europe, they are far rarer than those of the Bronze Age. The fact that so many of these mounds show heavy use in the Neolithic, and contain so many burial goods, shows a flourishing and unique culture once existed in East Riding during that period. It may even be argued that British round burial mounds, popular throughout the Bronze Age, saw their first adoption in this region during the Neolithic.

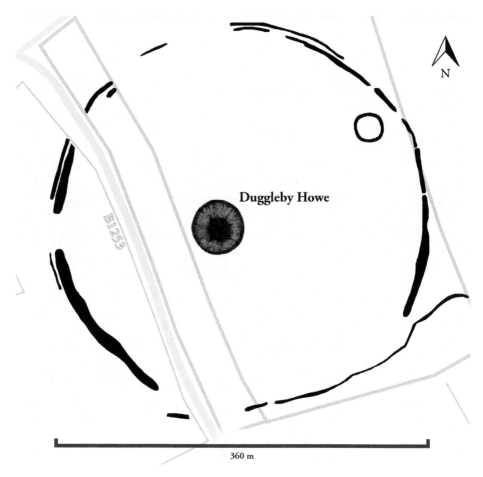

THE DITCHED ENCLOSURE SURROUNDING DUGGLEBY HOWE, AS SURVEYED BY IAN KINNES, 1983.

Finally, there is a giant concentric ditch encircling the mound, which appears as a crop mark during dry periods. It is a rough enclosure over 360m in diameter: larger than the modern village of Duggleby. There is no consensus as to what this enclosure was. It may be the remains of a super-henge, a causewayed enclosure or even a wholly unique monument alto-gether. Perhaps the most intriguing theory suggests the chalk used to create the mound in Phase 5 was sourced from the digging of this ditch. People would dig the trench, and gradually throw over 5,000 tons of spoil onto the mound. This is a similar theory to that given for Silbury Hill near Avebury, where multiple generations would slowly grow the mound, basket by basket.

WILLIE HOWE

TA 06161 72349

Willie Howe, the largest mound in East Riding, sits between Wold Newton and Burton Fleming. It was reopened to visitors in 2020 after Historic England had the trees and brambles on it pruned. Finding it is easy, as it stands proud on the horizon line, below the crest of a low hill overlooking Wold Newton to the west. Like the Rudston Monolith, Willie Howe sits only 200m from the Gypsey Race.

The mound has been investigated many times in the past. The first record of an excavation was in 1857, when the landowner, Lord Londesborough, unsuccessfully excavated the mound, failing to find anything before abandoning the dig. His dig did, however, determine that the mound was almost entirely made of chalk. Londesborough was unlikely to have been the first to dig into the mound, and it remains unknown if it was looted in the past. Nevertheless, William Greenwell dug into its centre in 1887. Of all the barrows he had explored, none confused him more than Willie Howe. Digging deep, he found an 'oval grave ... 4ft by 2ft 8 inches' (1.2 by 1m).

THE GOLDEN CUP LEGEND HAS ITS ROOTS IN THE EARLY BRONZE AGE.

Curiously, despite not having been disturbed, the grave was empty. This seems to have baffled Greenwell, who in all his years of digging graves had never come across such an empty cist. He wrote:

I had always disbelieved in the erection of such memorials as cenotaphs at the time when these barrows were constructed. That supposition appears, however, to be countenanced by the experience of this mound, and I am forced to admit the possibility that this very large mass of chalk stones was thrown up merely to commemorate, and not to contain the body of, some great personage.

The idea that Willie Howe was a cenotaph (an empty grave built for memorial purposes) is interesting, if fanciful. Britain's most famous prehistoric mound, Silbury Hill at Avebury, is similar and was also devoid of a grave. If such a monument existed here, it would be unusual and deserving of widespread study. However, there is reason to believe this mound, like all the great mounds, began as a Neolithic grave. If so, it would suggest only the deepest sections of the mound contain a body. Southside Mount and Duggleby Howe, for example, both had Neolithic graves cut under the mound. Also of note is a fragment of a polished stone axe head, found 130m south of the mound. Even if meagre in evidence, it seems Neolithic religious activity was taking place close to Willie Howe.

While this book does not detail folklore, there is an important myth surrounding Willie Howe. Twelfth-century folklorist William of Newburgh, famous for the stories 'The Anarchy' and 'The Green Children', wrote a curious tale about the mound. The story details a lone wanderer making his way down a country lane early one morning, his thoughts lost in the stillness of the valley. Suddenly, a faint flicker of light catches his eye, and he turns to see a cluster of tiny figures dancing on a mound ahead – Willie Howe.

As he approaches, he realises that these are not mere sprites, but a band of fairies plotting and scheming in the shadows. They beckon him forth with a wicked gleam in their eyes, offering him a drink from a golden cup. But this man is no fool. He takes the cup and pretends to take a sip, before running away with the cup clutched tightly in his hand. According to Newburgh, the fairies 'pursued him; but he escaped by the fleetness of his steed, and reached the village with his extraordinary prize'.

Believe it or not, this so-called 'Fairy Cup Legend' is common across Europe and may be based in archaeology. The story is almost always the same, concerning the theft of a golden cup from a group of fairies living within a burial mound. Such sites have therefore been known as fairy mounds in some regions, particularly Ireland, Wales and Cornwall.

The connection between elaborate drinking vessels and burial mounds is a rabbit hole in and of itself. Ornate cups have been unearthed from many burial mounds in the past. Examples from Britain include the Amber Hove Cup, the Rillaton Cup and the Ringlemere Cup. Each example was found in a large burial mound. In his 1877 compendium on prehistoric Barrows (aptly titled *British Barrows*), William Greenwell noted how several of these cups had been found in the Yorkshire Wolds.

SHARP HOWES CEMETERY AND THE FOLKTON DRUMS

TA 04936 77671

In the summer of 1868, William Greenwell made his greatest discovery. It was a find that not only cemented his legacy as one of England's foremost treasure hunters – but one that continues to perplex archaeologists over 100 years later.

The Folkton Drums are some of the most significant examples of prehistoric artwork ever discovered. Discovered in a Late Neolithic round barrow, these ornate chalk cylinders were found beside the skeleton of a 5-year-old child, arranged at their hips and head. Since their discovery, their decorations have been interpreted in many ways, from calendars and spirit vessels to measuring instruments. What is certain is that their placement represented something very personal to a family coming to terms with the loss of a beloved child. Sadly, grief is a timeless language.

In the process of digging the barrow's mound, Greenwell wiped it from existence. However, several burial mounds do still survive to the immediate west of the barrow's location. This collection, known as Sharp Howes, contains eight barrows of the Great Mound variety. Greenwell excavated these in the 1880s as well, finding little – only a single female burial and a small pot. After these final excavations, the barrows in the area were finally left alone, their treasures a singular mystery never to be seen again …

A SKETCH OF THE TOP OF THE BURTON AGNES DRUM.

That was until 2015, over a hundred years after the Folkton Drums' discovery. The so-called Burton Agnes Drum was unearthed 16km south of the Folkton Barrow, near the small village of Burton Agnes. The drum was unveiled just prior to the opening of the British Museum's 2022 'World of Stonehenge Exhibition', along with two other finds from the grave: a bone pin and a small chalk ball. There is much to discuss about this object, as it may be the greatest British Neolithic artefact yet discovered in the twenty-first century. However, as this book was written the same year as its unveiling, the author sadly has little to report aside from its existence.

What we know for certain, is that the Burton Agnes Drum is a highly decorated chalk object, even more so than the Folkton Drums. It is a similar shape and size to the Folkton Drums, with the same distinct rimmed top. It has several unfinished motifs on its top, along with three deep, crude cups in a uniform triangle. While the three Folkton Drums were buried with one child, the one Burton Agnes Drum was buried with three children.

WOLD NEWTON

TA 04833 72619

The Wold Newton Barrow is one of the canonical four Great Mounds of Yorkshire. It is the closest of the four to the Gypsey Race, located a mere 30m from the stream. You can find it just south-east of the village of Wold Newton, on private land east of Rainsburgh Lane. This is not an easy monument to view, as almost all viewpoints are blocked by hedgerows.

This is yet another massive barrow excavated by John Robert Mortimer, who named it Barrow 284. He found it to be comparable to Duggleby Howe. The monument began as a wooden structure, used to excarnate the dead. Excarnation was a process that involved leaving bodies open to the elements until only the skeleton was left. The bones were interred as skeletons, which were jumbled into a shaft. After this, the bones were simply covered with a low mound. Five skeletons were found in this original phase, buried alongside the remains of a pig and some Neolithic pottery.

Into this Neolithic mound, at least four more burials appear to have been inserted later. There were two crouched burials inserted around the edges of the mound, a cremated child and fragments of a semi-cremated skull. These were accompanied by many burial accessories: Neolithic arrowheads, flint tools, a deer antler and many frogs. That last item – frogs – was certainly a bizarre find. Like the earlier pig bones, these frogs may have been an offering of food, and the proximity of the Gypsey Race may suggest the barrow had an aquatic theme.

After these burials, it appears the Wold Newton Barrow was finished off like Duggleby Howe. A ditch was dug around the site, 100m in diameter, and the mound further built up, with over 100 tons of chalk added to it. The date on which these last stages occurred is not known for certain, but we can assume it was like Duggleby Howe – around the beginning of the Early Bronze Age.

> **Author's note:** The barrows at Wold Newton and Willy Howe represent just two surviving barrows in this region north of Rudston. Halfway between Wold Newton and Burton Fleming, to the north, there are countless fields of circular crop marks. These are likely the remains of round barrows just like those at Wold Newton, with an inner mound and an outer ditch. If you are interested in exploring these sites, you can easily do so from the comfort of any computer or phone. Any satellite map using imagery from 2018 will allow easy access to the crop marks in the region, as a heatwave in the UK fortuitously coincided with the aerial photography that year.

FOX HILL BARROW

TA 07603 61677

The Fox Hill Barrow sits in a crop field south-east of Ruston Parva. It can be viewed from the nearby road and layby, from the other end of the field to the north. It appears as a silhouette on the horizon, within the length of the field boundary to the south. The field is private, so access is restricted.

Although not typically associated with the Great Mounds, it is one of the largest in Yorkshire, measuring 4m high and 24m across at its widest diameter. Like the Great Mounds in the region, it is a large bowl barrow that likely had a concentric ditch around its perimeter. However, traces of a ditch or other nearby earthworks have been lost, as ploughing has combed the adjacent fields flat. This has caused the loss of the outer edge of the mound, so we may assume it was even larger than we see today.

The date of the Fox Hill Barrow has been debated. While it is ostensibly a Neolithic to Early Bronze Age bowl barrow, like the Great Mounds, some archaeologists believe it to be a Roman burial mound. The reason for this theory, as noted by English Heritage in 1994, was the mound's 'large size'. Of course, we know that large prehistoric bowl barrows are common in the

Wolds. However, there is good reason to believe this barrow was used by later people.

Like Southside Mount and Pudding Pie Hill, the Fox Hill Barrow may have been reused in the Anglo-Saxon period. This may explain its astounding level of preservation, having experienced at least 2,000 fewer years of erosion. Using Southside Mount as a template, we can assume the barrow's core dates to the Neolithic, while the mound itself belongs to the Early Bronze Age. The Romans or the Anglo-Saxons may have later remodelled and expanded on this.

To the north-east of the barrow is a curious crop mark: two parallel trenches aligned towards the south-west. This could be another cursus monument, just 3km south-west of Rudston. The ceremonial landscape at Rudston, as we understand it, may not be so neatly contained within the four known cursus earthworks and the monolith. Like the landscape surrounding the Thornborough Henges and Devil's Arrows, Neolithic ritual enclosures may extend all around this region, with only the best-preserved examples surviving.

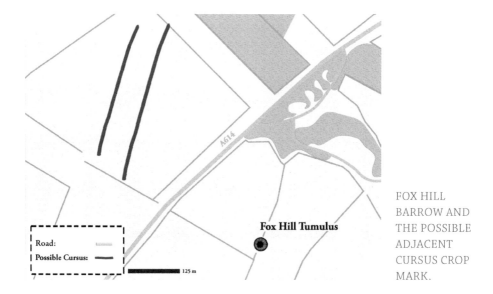

FOX HILL
BARROW AND
THE POSSIBLE
ADJACENT
CURSUS CROP
MARK.

Several more barrows were once present nearby. A barrow was excavated in the nineteenth century by John Robert Mortimer, only a mile to the east, at Ruston Parva. Inside the barrow, he found several semi-cremated bones piled into a hollowed-out log. Seven kilometres to the south-west, at Driffield, a barrow 18m in diameter was excavated by Lord Londesborough in 1851. Within the barrow, several cists were found containing crouched inhumations, dating to the Neolithic and Early Bronze Age, much like the other Great Barrows of East Riding. The same year, he excavated more large barrows to the south-west, at the village of Londesborough. He stated of these barrows: 'They number between thirty and forty in space not more than a mile across. Some of them are of great size, varying in height from two to eleven or twelve feet.'

THE PADDOCK HILL ENCLOSURE (LOST)

TA 03000 70700

Despite only appearing on rare occasions as a faint stain in the earth, the Paddock Hill Enclosure remains a fascinating site. It sits 2½km south-east of Wold Newton Mound and 3km from Willy Howe. Venturing to the site is not possible, as it is on private land. Moreover, doing so is futile, as nothing remains at ground level.

Archaeologist T.G. Manby conducted excavations at the site between 1973 and 1987, uncovering some of its history. During the mid to late Neolithic period, the first significant phase of construction occurred, which involved creating a Class II henge. The henge consisted of a circular ditch with a chalk bank on the exterior, aligned north-west to south-east. In 1975, Manby found a flake from a polished axe just north of the enclosure. The stone used to make the axe likely originated from the Langdale Valley in the Lake District.

Activity at the henge continued beyond the Neolithic period. Archaeologists uncovered fragments of Early Bronze Age pottery, including beaker sherds, near the henge. This activity was further evidenced by the remains of flint tools and food vessels, possibly signs of settlement. Later, during the mid-Bronze Age, it was extensively remodelled. The builders erected a 17m-wide timber circle around a central pit (which was found to contain an urn) and recut the ditch of the henge. This arrangement may have represented the conversion of the enclosure into a large burial circle of some sort, with posts surrounding a mound. This may have been comparable to Duggleby Howe.

For over a thousand years, the enclosure lay abandoned. Nevertheless, around AD 700 the Anglo-Saxons stumbled upon and resettled the site. They re-established a cemetery within the enclosure and reinforced the ditch with a palisade. Timber buildings sprang up all around, suggesting there was continuous occupation from the eighth to the ninth, and later thirteenth, centuries.

The excavations at Paddock Hill represent some of the best archaeology Britain has to offer. By the end of Manby's study, Mesolithic, Neolithic, Bronze Age, Roman, Anglo-Saxon and Norman artefacts had been recovered from in and around this 60m-wide enclosure, all of which only survives as a crop mark during sunny periods – uncommon in England. Truly, a rare and wonderful place.

T.G. Manby, who prefers to go by his initials, is something of an unsung hero of northern English archaeology. Authoring many important articles on Yorkshire and Derbyshire throughout the twentieth and twenty-first centuries, Manby's work was vital to the research of this book, as well as my previous one on Cumbria.

OTHER SITES IN EAST RIDING

Surprisingly, outside Rudston and the Four Great Mounds, there remain few tangible prehistoric monuments in East Riding. Standing stones are a rarity here, as are burial cairns, rock art panels and henges. Many of the monuments in the region survive in vast barrow cemeteries. Some of these stand proud in the landscape, while others reveal themselves only as crop marks.

As East Riding is covered with crop fields, the likelihood of gaining access to these barrows is slim. Thankfully, most survive on roadsides, so seeing them remains a possibility.

ACKLAM WOLD CEMETERY

There is an expansive complex of burial mounds east of the hamlet of Aldro, along a natural ridgeline overlooking Acklam. Most of these are only slight, having been ploughed away since the eighteenth century. Luckily (or unluckily, depending on who you ask), John Robert Mortimer excavated a number of these soon after their destruction, recording his finds in detail. Very few barrows in the area remain untouched. Only a single barrow survives in the landscape, east of Stone Sleights Farm (SE 80250 61692).

Among the most important of these mounds was Hanging Grimston, a long barrow like the example at Willerby Wold, with two linear ditches forming a wedge. Inside the barrow, the disarticulated bones of an adult were found, alongside several post holes containing burned wood. Unfortunately, the significance of this excavation is not fully understood, as Mortimer incorrectly believed a substantial portion of the long barrow was a dwelling, describing his finds as such. Subsequent radiocarbon dates, performed on pig remains found within the barrow, confirmed a date of burial between 3000 BC and 2760 BC.

There have been many Neolithic and Early Bronze Age artefacts discovered in the area surrounding Acklam Wold Cemetery. A polished stone axe, originating from the Lake District, was discovered nearby in Aldro. Two mace heads (ovular toolheads of unknown usage) made of quartz stone were also

LEFT: THE
ALDRO
EARTHWORKS.

BELOW: STONE
SLEIGHTS
BOWL BARROW.

ALDRO

STONE SLEIGHTS
BARROW

500 m

Dyke:

Barrows:

N

found in Aldro and are currently held at Hull Museum. A second polished axe was found just south of the Acklam Wold Cemetery mounds, this one unfinished and possibly deposited as a burial offering.

Aldro itself is quite an archaeological hotbed. The Aldro Earthworks form a border around a natural spur, with two large dykes cutting off the village to the north and south-east. Within its boundary are around nineteen Bronze Age barrows, all of which are only evident as crop marks. Any connection between these earthworks and the Acklam Wold Cemetery is uncertain, but it can be assumed that at least a thousand years separated these features.

CALLIS WOLD CEMETERY

SE 82180 57021

The Callis Wold Cemetery sprawls 5km south across Acklam Wold. It consisted of at least seven barrows, evenly spaced around the brow of a slight hill overlooking Kirkby Underdale to the north-west. I have given each barrow a letter, from A to G, which you can see labelled on the map provided. Just scanning over the area using a satellite map makes it easy to identify even more barrows via crop marks, including several Neolithic long barrows. However, only two barrows have survived: **A** and **B**.

Some of the barrows were excavated by J.R. Mortimer in the nineteenth century. **Barrow C**, also known as Hollies Barrow, was the largest barrow at the site. It had already been partially covered by the road by 1868, and now no longer survives at all. However, you can still see evidence of it in the curved shape of the treeline where it once sat. Two smashed urns were found south of the centre of the barrow. Nine jewellery beads, made from jet and dark shale, were placed within one of these.. Two crouched inhumations, both buried off-centre, may have been the primary burials at the site.

Barrow D was excavated in 1864, by which time it was already hard to discern due to plough damage. It was originally around 8m in diameter. Within the centre of the barrow, a pit was found containing a single cremation alongside a honed flint. North of the centre, a small cist was discovered. Although very disturbed by the plough, the cist was found to contain the

CALLIS WOLD A.

bones of a child, next to which a pot had been placed. **Barrow F** was excavated in both 1864 and 1892. Several cremations were buried in pits inside, one in an urn and another directly into the ground. Alongside these, a small burned cup, burned cloth and several flint tools were found. Interestingly, several flint arrowheads were found, some leaf-shaped, dating to the Neolithic, and some barbed, dating to the Early Bronze Age.

Barrow E was excavated in 1874, when it was around 10m in diameter. A grave containing three bodies was found inside the barrow, beside which fragments of pottery and pieces of unshaped flint were found. These bodies were the earliest in the grave, and likely dated to either the Neolithic or Early Bronze Age. A later burial urn was also discovered within the mound, on top of which a bronze dagger and a small pot, known as an incense cup, were found.

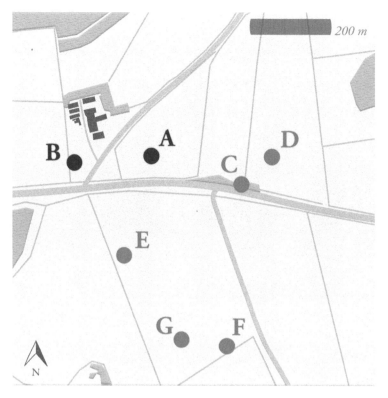

LOCATION OF
THE CALLIS
WOLD
BARROWS.

Author's note: Another collection of barrows lies 1km east of the Callis Wold Cemetery, following the same alignment across the natural ridgeline overlooking Kirkby Underdale. These too were excavated by Mortimer and were found to contain similar artefacts dating to the Neolithic and Early Bronze Age. The surviving examples at this site are more overgrown than those at Callis Wold but appear to be better preserved under their bushy exterior.

Between this collection, and those at the Callis Wold Cemetery, is a 450m-long dyke, dividing the landscape between the two. However, there is little distinction between the barrows here, and those at Acklam Wold. The pattern of barrows and dykes continues between the two, across the eastern ridgeline of the Wolds. It is highly comparable to the pattern seen at Cleave Dyke (see Chapter 1), where a boundary, originally formed with Neolithic and Early Bronze Age barrows, was later re-delineated using vast dykes in the mid-Bronze and Iron Ages.

WILLERBY WOLD LONG BARROW

TA 02958 76078

Willerby Wold Long Barrow only survives as a slight earthwork. It sits at the top of a small hill to the north-west of Fordon, overlooking swathes of Wold countryside. As this is an Early Neolithic site (est. 3600 BC), the surrounding area was probably at least partially forested. Situating a burial mound on such a hill, deforested to form a crest, would have provided the site with a wonderful sense of scale.

The barrow was excavated between 1958 and 1960, revealing that it was built upon a mortuary enclosure, where bodies were dressed before burial. Such sites are common across England, with other examples being found in Cumbria and Wiltshire. Rarer was a later 'ritual pit' built on the barrow's eastern edge, where bodies were cremated. This was similar to the feature found within Hanging Grimston Long Barrow, suggesting these sites belong to a subset of monuments known as crematorium long barrows.

SKIPSEA CASTLE

TA 16202 55080

Skipsea Castle is unusual. Like several other sites listed in this book (see Catterick, Chapter 2), what was at first thought to be a medieval motte-and-bailey castle (est. 1086) was later revealed to be prehistoric. A 2016 excavation of the site, led by archaeologist Jim Leary, showed that the core of the mound dated to around 500 BC – the Iron Age.

There is plenty left to learn about the mound, and as it is not definitively a 'prehistoric monument' it may not belong in this book at all. As of early 2023, excavations are planned at the site, when much will likely be revealed.

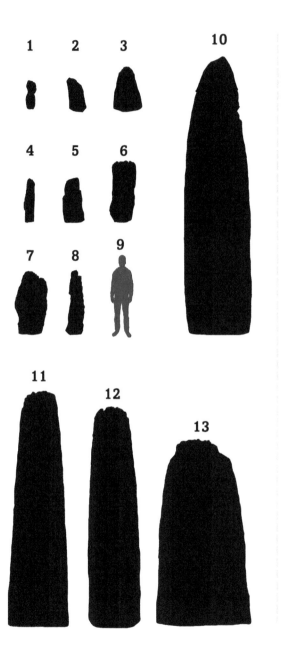

1. Old Wife's Neck

2. Crown End Stone Row

3. Nine Stones

4. Simon Howe Stone Row

5. Turtley Hole Stones

6. Wade Stone South

7. Blakey Topping

8. High Bride Stones

9. Average Adult

10. The Rudston Monolith

11. Devil's Arrows Central

12. Devil's Arrows South

13. Devil's Arrows North

NATIONAL GRID REFERENCES

NORTH YORK MOORS

The Lord Stones	NZ 52368 02980
Nab Ridge Bride Stones	SE 57565 97908
Drake Howe	NZ 53754 02959
Three Thumb Stone	NZ 52542 01686
The Wainstones 1	NZ 55630 03595
The Wainstones 3	NZ 55581 03443
The Wainstones 5	NZ 55800 03636
The Wainstones 6	NZ 55841 03338
Simon Howe	SE 83008 98096
The Old Wife's Neck	NZ 90067 02140
Hazel Head Stone Row	SE 80698 99660
High Bridestones	NZ 85027 04614
Low Bridestones	NZ 84575 04869
Ramsdale Stones	NZ 92059 03776
Breckon Howe	NZ 85377 03407
Saltergate Moor Stone Row	SE 86487 95746
Newgate Foot Stones	SE 87191 93380
Harwood Dale Circle	SE 98241 96983
Three Howes (Fylingdales)	SE 96601 98030
Cloughton Moor Stone Circle	TA 00380 95947
York Museum Garden Stone	SE 59971 52096
Raven Hall Hotel	NZ 98067 01786
Danby Rigg Ring Cairn A	NZ 70798 06573

Danby Dykes	NZ 70773 06062
Old Wife Stone (Danby Rigg)	NZ 71039 05925
Danby Rigg Pits	NZ 70670 06179
Commondale Stone Circle	NZ 63779 10855
North Ings Stone Row	NZ 64498 12019
Crown End Stone Row	NZ 66065 07112
Old Castle Hill Stone Row	NZ 67361 12016
Great Ayton Bank Cairn	NZ 59377 11488
Siss Cross Hill Enclosure	NZ 69999 11063
Dimmingdale Enclosure	NZ 68588 11877
Greenwell's Long Barrow	SE 49156 90337
Boltby Scar Hill Fort	SE 50628 85653
Nine Stones Row	SE 47078 95310
Scarth Wood Moor Cemetery	SE 46856 99959
Howe Hill	SE 46738 84623
Newton Mulgrave Long Barrow	NZ 77613 14327
Cucket Stone	NZ 82509 09056
Wade Stone North	NZ 82953 14414
Wade Stones South	NZ 83050 13009
Rabbit Hill Barrow	SE 41417 96865
Cammon Stone	SE 62676 99997
Three Howes (Cockayne Ridge)	SE 63233 98176
The Blackpark Stone	SE 75250 90932
Swarth Howe Stone Row	NZ 84209 08931
North Riding Forest – Fox Howes	SE 90264 90954
North Riding Forest – Three Howes	SE 90327 90645
North Riding Forest – Brown Howes	SE 89707 90842
North Riding Forest – Scamridge Farm Long Barrow	SE 89201 86055
Harland Moor Stone Circle	SE 67527 92610
Studfold Ring	SE 58128 79864
Roseberry Stone	NZ 57032 13054
Allan Tofts Rock Art	NZ 83000 03000
Bog House Stone	SE 65508 93297
Helmsley Barrows	SE 62191 83768

VALES OF MOWBRAY AND YORK

The Thornborough Henges	SE 28522 79462
Devil's Arrows	SE 39101 66534
Cana Barn Henge	SE 36091 71875
Tenlands Earthwork	SE 36419 71319
Low Barn Henge	SE 35252 73542
Dishforth Henge	SE 37023 72606
Nunwick Henge	SE 37023 72606
Stapley Hill Round Barrow	SE 32322 81657
Sinderby Henge	SE 34307 81086
Pudding Pie Hill	SE 43697 81028
Blois Hall Cairn	SE 34812 72413
Hutton Conyers Cairn	SE 35301 74335
Catterick Palisaded Enclosure	SE 25180 96840
Pallot Hill	SE 23960 98042
Catterick Henge	SE 22973 98552
Newton Kyme Henge	SE 45890 44988
Hartwith Moor Stone	SE 21235 62741
Dacre Banks Rock Art	SE 18601 61645
Gilling Long Barrow	SE 60172 74169

THE DALES AND CRAVEN

Maiden Castle	SE 02185 98101
Swale Hall Bowl Barrow	SE 03992 98523
Harkerside Circle	SE 03534 97610
Addlebrough Cairn	SD 94600 88124
Stoney Raise	SD 95062 86914
Ox Close Stone Circle	SD 99002 90132
Thackthwaite Beck Stone Circle	SD 98912 91211
Castle Dykes	SD 98228 87289
Yockenthwaite Stone Circle	SD 89977 79363
Druid's Altar (Bordley Circle)	SD 94946 65275
Yarnbury Henge	SE 01406 65417

Skirehorns Potential Henge A	SD 96995 64441
Skirehorns Potential Henge B	SD 96484 64683
Fancarl Top Stone Circle	SE 06432 63052
Threshfield Henges (lost)	SD 98763 64253
Kilnsey Stone Circle	SD 95124 68034
Hanging Stones Rock	SE 12822 46766
Twelve Apostles	SE 12610 45066
Grubstones Stone Circle	SE 13648 44722
Swastika Stone	SE 09560 46972
Planet Stone	SE 12961 46398
Backstone Beck Stone Circle	SE 12597 46139
Backstone Beck Rock Art	SE 12738 46251
Haystack Rock	SE 13027 46314
Idol Stone	SE 13265 45946
Great Skirtful of Stones	SE 14056 44547
Little Skirtful of Stones	SE 13831 45190
Badger Stone	SE 11076 46052
Barmishaw Stone	SE 11194 46420
Panorama Stone	SE 11475 47298
Willy Hall's Woods Stone	SE 11589 46626
Bradup Stone Circle (lost)	SE 08950 43900
King's Cairn	SE 00924 47563
Queen's Cairn	SE 00873 47537
Hamblethorpe Stones	SE 00304 47627
Farnhill Rock Art	SE 00639 47104
Apronful of Stones	SD 80653 66195
Sheep Scar Circle	SD 80517 66476
Celtic Walls	SD 80086 67417
Giggleswick Scar Ring Cairn	SD 79798 67471
Apron Full of Stones (Gragareth)	SD 70915 78809
Soldier's Trench	SE 13052 39106
Hare Hill Ring Cairn	SD 92954 47698
West Agra Rock Art	SE 14239 81749
Ewden Beck	SK 23810 96640

Todmorden Monoliths	SD 92521 23598
Turtley Holes Stones	SD 99833 22367
Brown Hills Beck Tumuli	SD 75640 60241
Harden Moor Stone Circle	SE 07497 38678
Cottingley Woods Rock Art	SE 09773 37857
Tree of Life Motif	SE 18016 50603

EAST RIDING AND THE YORKSHIRE WOLDS

Rudston Cursus A Terminal	TA 09981 65810
Rudston Monolith	TA 09805 67744
Rudston Beacon	TA 09484 65622
Southside Mount	TA 10756 66580
Duggleby Howe	SE 88051 66893
Willie Howe	TA 06161 72349
Sharpe Howes Cemetery	TA 04936 77671
Wold Newton	TA 04833 72619
Fox Hill Barrow	TA 07603 61677
Paddock Hill Enclosure	TA 03000 70700
Stone Sleights Farm Barrow	SE 80250 61692
Callis Wold Cemetery	SE 82180 57021
Willerby Wold Long Barrow	TA 02958 76078
Skipsea Castle	TA 16202 55080

BIBLIOGRAPHY

Adams, R.L., 'Household Ethnoarchaeology and Social Action in a Megalith-Building Society in West Sumba, Indonesia', *Asian Perspectives*, 58(2), pp.331–365 (2019).

Archaeology Data Service, 'Thornborough Henges: Air Photo Mapping Project', Archaeological Services WYAS (2006).

Archaeology Data Service, 'The Prehistoric Rock Art of England: Recording, managing and enjoying our carved heritage', PDF, English Heritage, Northumberland County Council (2008).

Archaeology Services Durham, 'Maiden Castle and West Hagg, Swaledale, North Yorkshire', Report 2631 (2011).

Bailey, J., 'Willy Howe. British Folklore'. Retrieved 26 January 2022 from http://britishfolklore.com/willy-howe (n.d.).

Beex, W., & Peterson, J., 'The Arminhall Henge in Space and Time: How Virtual Reality Contributes to Research on its Orientation', PDF (2004).

Bennett, P., *Twelve Apostles Stone Circle, West Yorkshire*, Northern Antiquarian Publications (2017).

Berger, J.-F., & Guilaine, J., 'The 8200calBP Abrupt Environmental Change and the Neolithic Transition: A Mediterranean Perspective', *Quaternary International: The Journal of the International Union for Quaternary Research*, 200(1), pp.31–49 (2009).

Bonsall, C., et al., 'Climate Change and the Adoption of Agriculture in North-West Europe', *European Journal of Archaeology*, 5(1), pp.9–23 (2002).

Bradford Telegraph and Argus, 'Mystery Surrounds Vanishing Circle', www.the-telegraphandargus.co.uk/news/8080170.mystery-surrounds-vanishing-circle (31 January 1998).

Brown, H.J., 'Understanding the Later Prehistoric Field Systems of the Yorkshire Dales', PhD Thesis, University of Bradford (2016).

Brück, J., & Fokkens, 'H., Bronze Age Settlements', in H.F.A. Harding (ed.), *The Oxford Handbook of the European Bronze Age*, Oxford University Press (2013).

Brück, J., & Goodman, M., *Making Places in the Prehistoric World: Themes in Settlement Archaeology*, Taylor & Francis Group (1999).

Cassidy, L.M., et al., 'A Dynastic Elite in Monumental Neolithic Society', *Nature* (2020).

Chapman, H.P., 'Rethinking the "Cursus Problem" – Investigating the Neolithic Landscape Archaeology of Rudston, East Yorkshire, UK, Using GIS', *Proceedings of the Prehistoric Society*, 71, pp.159–170 (2005).

Chappell, G., & Brown, P., *Prehistoric Rock Art in the North York Moors*, History Press (2012).

Clare, T., 'A re-interpretation of the Levens Park ring cairn, Cumbria, based on the original excavation archives', *The Archaeological Journal* (2021).

Cockrell, T., 'Prehistoric Rock-Art at Spout House Hill, South Yorkshire', Bolsterstone Archaeology and Heritage Group report (2020).

Colls, J.N.M., 'Letter Upon Some Early Remains Discovered in Yorkshire', in *Archaeologia, or Miscellaneous Tracts Relating to Antiquity*, pp.299–307 (1845).

Collyer, R., *Ilkley, Ancient and Modern*, Forgotten Books, 2018 Reprint (1885).

Cummings, L.B., 'Rethinking the henge monuments of the British Isles', PhD Thesis, Newcastle University (2019).

Powlesland, D., et al., 'Archaeological Excavations at Roulston Scar, North York Moors National Park', The Landscape Research Centre (2013).

Darvill, T., 'Monuments and Monumentality in Bronze Age Europe', in H.F.A. Harding (ed.), *The Oxford Handbook of the European Bronze Age*, Oxford University Press (2013).

Deegan, A., 'Prehistoric Monuments in the A1 Corridor, Young Archaeologists' Club', *The Thornborough Trust Booklet*, CBA.

Dickinson, S., 'Between the mountains and the sea: a new monument complex on the Cumbrian coast', in *PAST Newsletter of the Prehistoric Society,* No. 100, The Prehistoric Society (2022).

'Earth and Sky: The Thornborough Henge Monument Complex', *Current Archaeology*, the-past.com (25 May 2014).

Eastmead, S., & Laurie, T., 'Ellerton Moor Juniper Rigg: A Bronze Age landscape revealed by a recent heather burn', Swaledale and Arkengarthdale Archaeology Group (2015).

Elgee, F., *Early Man in North-East Yorkshire*, John Bellows (1930).

Evans, H., *Neolithic and Bronze Age Landscapes of Cumbria*, BAR British Series, 463 (2008).

Fairén-Jiménez, S., 'British Neolithic Rock Art in its Landscape', *Journal of Field Archaeology*, 32(3), pp.283–295 (2007).

Faull, M.L., & Moorhouse, S.A., *West Yorkshire: An Archaeological Survey to A.D. 1500* , West Yorkshire Metropolitan Council (1981).

Ferraby, R., & Millett, M., *Isurium Brigantum: An Archaeological Survey of Roman Aldborough*, Society of Antiquaries of London (2020).

Frank, G., *Ryedale and North Yorkshire Antiquities*, York: Sampson Brothers (1888).

Garrow, D., Griffiths, S., Anderson-Whymark, H., et al., 'Stepping Stones to the Neolithic? Radiocarbon Dating the Early Neolithic on Islands Within the "Western Seaways" of Britain, *Proceedings of the Prehistoric Society* 83, Cambridge University Press, pp.97–135 (2017).

Gerrard, J., 'The Ancient East Yorkshire Monument that's Home to Drunken Fairies', retrieved 26 January 2022 from www.hulldailymail.co.uk/news/hull-east-yorkshire-news/east-yorkshire-monument-drunken-fairies-4613368 (18 October 2020).

Gibson, A., et al., 'Survey and Excavation at the Henges of the Wharfe Valley, North Yorkshire, 2013–15', *Archaeological Journal*, 175(1), pp.1–54 (2018).

Gibson, A.M., *Enclosing the Neolithic: Recent Studies in Britain and Europe*, Archaeopress (2012).

Gibson, A., Bayliss, A., Heard, H., Mainland, I., Ogden, A.R., Ramsey, C.B., Cook, G., van der Plicht, J., & Marshall, P., 'Recent Research at Duggleby Howe, North Yorkshire', *Archaeological Journal*, 166(1), pp.39–78 (2009).

Gibson, A., 'Space and Episodic Ritual at the Monumental Neolithic Round Mound of Duggleby Howe, North Yorkshire, England', *Préhistoires Méditerranéennes*, Colloque (2014).

Gillings, M., & Pollard, J., 'Making Megaliths: Shifting and Unstable Stones in the Neolithic of the Avebury Landscape', *Cambridge Archaeological Journal*, 26(4), pp.537–559 (2016).

Greenwell, W., *British Barrows: A Record of the Examination of Sepulchral Mounds in Various Parts of England*, Oxford, Clarendon Press (1877).

Greenwell, W.I., 'Recent Researches in Barrows in Yorkshire, Wiltshire, Berkshire, etc', *Archaeologia*, 52(1), pp.1–72 (1890).

Halkon, P., Healey, E., et al., 'Change and Continuity Within the Prehistoric Landscape of the Foulness Valley, East Yorkshire' (2).

Hale, D., Platell, A., & Millard, A., 'A Late Neolithic Palisaded Enclosure at Marne Barracks, Catterick, North Yorkshire', *Proceedings of the Prehistoric Society*, 75, pp.265–304 (2009).

Harding, A.F., et al., 'Prehistoric and early medieval activity on Danby Rigg, north Yorkshire', *Archaeological Journal*, 151(1), pp.16–97 (2013).

Harding, A.F. et al., 'Prehistoric and Early medieval Activity on Danby Rigg, North Yorkshire', *Archaeological Journal*, vol. 151, pp.16–97 (1994).

Harding, J., 'Interpreting The Neolithic: The Monuments of North Yorkshire', *Oxford Journal of Archaeology*, Vol. 16, Iss. 3, pp.279–295 (1994).

Harding, J., *Thornborough, North Yorkshire: Neolithic and Bronze-Age Monument Complex*, York: Archaeology Data Service (2008).

Hawkes, J., *A Guide to the Prehistoric and Roman Monuments in England and Wales*, Chatto & Windus (1951).

Hedges, J.D., & Buckley, D.G., *Springfield Cursus: And the Cursus Problem*, Essex County Council (1981).

Heyd, V., 'Europe 2500 to 2200 BC: Between Expiring Ideologies and Emerging Complexity', in H.F.A. Harding (ed.), *The Oxford Handbook of the European Bronze Age*, Oxford University Press (2013).

Historic England, 'Prehistoric Avenues and Alignments: Introductions to Heritage Assets', HEAG 216 (2016).

Jamieson, E., Stastney, P., & Leary, J., 'Dating Skipsea Mound, East Yorkshire', Yorkshire Archaeological and Historical Society (2019).

Johnston, R.A., 'Land and Society: The Bronze Age Cairn-fields and Field Systems of Britain', Dept. of Archaeology, University of Newcastle upon Tyne, PhD Dissertation (2001).

Jones, A., et al., 'Digital Imaging and Prehistoric Imagery: A New Analysis of the Folkton Drums', *Antiquity*, 89(347), pp.1083–1095 (2015).

Keen, L., & Radley, J., 'Report on the Petrological Identification of Stone Axes from Yorkshire', *Proceedings of the Prehistoric Society*, 37(1), pp.16–37 (2014).

Langdale, J., & T., *A Topographical Dictionary of Yorkshire: Containing the Names of All the Towns, Villages, Hamlets, Gentlemen's Seats, &c. in the County of York. A Brief History of Places Most Remarkable for Antiquities, Biographical Notices of Eminent Persons*, second edition (1822).

Londesborough, 'An account of the Opening of some Tumuli in the East Riding of Yorkshire by the Right Hon. The Lord Londesborough, FSA, *Archaeologia, or Miscellaneous Tracts, Relating to Antiquity*, Vol. 34, Iss. 2 (1852).

Loveday, R., 'Cursuses and Related Monuments of the British Neolithic', PhD Thesis, University of Leicester (1985).

Loveday, R., 'From Ritual to Riches – the Route to Individual Power in Later Neolithic Eastern Yorkshire?' in Barclay, G. & Brophy K., *Defining a Regional Neolithic: Evidence from Britain and Ireland*, Oxford, England: Oxbow Books (2009).

Loveday, R., *Inscribed Across the Landscape: The Cursus Enigma*, Tempus Publishing (2006).

Manby, T.G., Halkon, P., et al., 'Neolithic Settlement Evidence form Hayton, East Yorks', *Yorkshire Archaeological Journal*, 82, Iss. 1 (2010).

Manby, T.G., Moorhouse, S., & Ottaway, P., 'The Archaeology of Yorkshire: An Assessment at the Beginning of the Twenty-First Century: Papers Arising Out of the Yorkshire Archaeological Resource Framework Forum Conference at Ripon, September, 1998', Yorkshire Archaeological Society (2003).

Manby, T.G., 'The Distribution of Rough-Cut, "Cumbrian" Stone Axes', *Transactions of the Cumberland & Westmorland Antiquarian & Archaeological Society*, 65: 2 (1965).

Martlew, R.D., & Ruggles, C.L.N., 'Ritual and Landscape on the West Coast of Scotland', *Proceedings of the Prehistoric Society*, Vol. 62. (1996).

Martlew, R.D., 'The Druids' Altar: A "Scottish" Stone Circle in Craven, North Yorkshire', *Yorkshire Archaeological Journal* (2010).

Mellor Archaeological Trust – 'Shaw Cairn'. Accessed at www.mellorarchaeology. org.uk/shaw-cairn.html, 3 November 2013).

Mortimer, J.R., 'An Account of the Opening of the Tumulus, Howe Hill, Duggleby', *Proceedings of the Yorkshire Geological and Polytechnic Society*, 12(2), pp.215–225 (1892).

Mortimer, J.R., *Forty Years Research in British and Saxon Burial Mounds of East Yorkshire*, A. Brown and Sons (1905).

Olalde, I., Brace, S., Allentoft, M., et al., 'The Beaker phenomenon and the genomic transformation of north-west Europe', *Nature* (2018).

Oswald, A., 'Prehistoric Linear Boundary Earthworks: Introductions to Heritage Assets', Historic England (2018).

Paulsson, B.S., 'Radiocarbon dates and Bayesian modeling support maritime diffusion model for megaliths in Europe', PNAS, Department of Historical Studies, University of Gothenburg (2018).

Pierpoint, S., 'Three Radiocarbon Dates for Yorkshire Prehistory', *Antiquity*, 53(209), pp.224–225 (1979).

Pollard, J., '"These Places Have Their Moments": Thoughts on Settlement Practices in the British Neolithic', in Brück, J., & Goodman, M., *Making Places in the Prehistoric World: Themes in Settlement Archaeology*, Taylor & Francis Group (1999).

Powlesland, D., et al., 'Archaeological Excavations at Roulston Scar, North York Moors National Park', The Landscape Research Centre (2013).

Raistrick, A., 'The Bronze Age in West Yorkshire', *Yorkshire Archaeological Journal*, 29, pp.354–365 (1929).

Ruddiman, W.F., & Ellis, E.C, 'Effect of per-capita land use changes on Holocene forest clearance and CO_2 emissions', *Quaternary Science Reviews*, 28(27), pp.3011–3015 (2009).

Sanderson, D., 'Decorated chalk drum is hailed as the most important prehistoric art find in Britain for 100 years', *The Times*, retrieved 10 February 2022, from www. thetimes.co.uk/article/decorated-chalk-drum-is-hailed-as-the-most -important-prehistoric-art-find-in-britain-for-100-years-007v25jq3

Smith, B.A. & Walker, A.A., *Rock Art & Ritual: Mindscapes of Prehistory*, Amberley, second edition (2013).

Speight, H., *The Craven and North-West Yorkshire Highlands*, Smith Settle, new edition (1 May 1989, original print, 1892).

Spratt, D.A., 'Linear Earthworks on the Tabular Hills, North-East Yorkshire', Sheffield, *Department of Archaeology and Prehistory, Monograph* (1989).

Spratt, D.A. & Simmons, I.G., 'Prehistoric Activity and Environment on the North York Moors', *Journal of Archaeological Science*, Vol. 3, Iss. 3 (1976).

Spratt, D.A., 'Recent British Research on Prehistoric Territorial Boundaries', *Journal of World Prehistory* 5(4), Springer: pp.439–480 (1991).

Stone, J. & Clowes, M., 'Wildfire and Archaeological Research on Fylingdales Moor', *Prehistoric Yorkshire*, 55, English Heritage (2006).

Swali P, Schulting R, Gilardet A, et al. (2023) Yersinia pestis genomes reveal plague in Britain 4000 years ago. *Nature Communications* 14(1): 2930.

Tilley, C., 'The Powers of Rocks: Topography and Monument Construction on Bodmin Moor', *World Archaeology*, 28(2), pp.161–176 (1996).

Tissiman, J., 'Report on Excavations in Barrows, in Yorkshire, by Mr. John Tissiman of Scarborough Communicated by Lord Londesborough', *Journal of The British Archaeological Association* (1851).

Turner, T.S., *History of Aldborough and Boroughbridge: Containing an Account of the Roman Antiquities, Devil's Arrows, Churches, Halls, and Other Curiosities*, A. Hall, Virtue, and Company (1853).

Valdez-Tullett, J., *Design and Connectivity: The Case of Atlantic Rock Art*, BAR Publishing (2019).

Vyner, B., 'A New Context for Rock Art: A Late Neolithic and Early Bronze Age Ritual Monument at Stoupe Brow, Fylingdales, North Yorkshire', *Proceedings of the Prehistoric Society*, Vol. 77 (2011).

Vyner, B., 'Cross-Ridge Boundaries on Fylingdales Moor', John Cross Rigg & Latter Gate Hills', *Prehistoric Yorkshire,* 58 (2021).

Vyner, B., et al., 'Moorland Monuments: Studies in the Archaeology of North-East Yorkshire in Honour of Raymond Hayes and Don Spratt', *CBA Research Report 101*, York: Council for British Archaeology, pp.5–15 (1995).

Waddington, C., 'Cup and Ring Marks in Context', *Cambridge Archaeological Journal*, 8(1), pp.29–53 (1998).

Walker, R., 'The Devil's Arrows Boroughbridge Town Council Leaflet', Boroughbridge & District Historical Society (n.d.).

Weldrake, D., 'Haystack Rock Ilkley Moor: A Tourist's Guide to Interesting Archaeological Sites in West Yorkshire', West Yorkshire Archaeology Advisory Service (2010).

Wessex Archaeology, 'Loch Migdale, Sutherland, Highlands, Scotland Archaeological Evaluation and an Assessment of the Results', Channel 4 *Time Team* Excavation (2003).

White, W., *A Month in Yorkshire* (1861). Accessible at www.gutenberg.org/files/35933/35933-h/35933-h.htm

WEB PAGES

Historic England's Aerial Archaeology Mapping Explorer, https://historicengland.org.uk/research/results/aerial-archaeology-mapping-explorer

The Journal of Antiquities, www.thejournalofantiquities.com

Out of Oblivion, www.outofoblivion.org.uk

Scottish Heritage Database, Canmore, www.canmore.org.uk/thesaurus

The Stone Rows of Great Britain, an excellent database of stone rows, www.stonerows.wordpress.com

Yorkshire Archaeological Aerial Mapping, yaamapping.co.uk

PRAISE FOR YORKSHIRE'S PREHISTORIC MONUMENTS

'Adam has compiled the best kind of field guide to the prehistoric wonders of northern England – one as inspirational and revelatory as it is informative. Meticulously described in words and pictures, whole ceremonial landscapes from the Neolithic and Bronze Age are uncovered in these pages which I'd never otherwise have known about. After only five minutes leafing through the book I was making plans for a trip north!'

David R. Abram, artist, aerial photographer and author of *Aerial Atlas of Ancient Britain.*

'This book is a must-have for all history-lovers, stone-hunters and archaeological detectives. A celebration of the fascinating but often overlooked prehistoric monuments and landscapes of Yorkshire, written with precision, expertise and passion. If you've ever felt the urge to hike across a wind-blasted moor in search of rock art or remote cairns, you need this book. From barrows to stone rows, engraved outcrops to massive monoliths, this is a crash course in landscape archaeology and a comprehensive gazetteer of sites (including the ones that are fiendish to locate). Simple maps help you locate sites, clear diagrams and descriptions indicate what you're looking for and aerial photos put it all into a wider context. A joy – both in the field, and from the comfort of your armchair.'

Mary-Ann Ochota, TV presenter / broadcaster & author of *Secret Britain and Hidden Histories: A Spotter's Guide to the British Landscape*